SOBER
DAD

SOBER DAD

THE MANUAL FOR PERFECTLY IMPERFECT PARENTING

Michael Graubart

Hazelden
Publishing

Hazelden Publishing
Center City, Minnesota 55012
hazelden.org/bookstore

ISBN: 978-1-61649-700-2

Library of Congress Cataloging-in-Publication Data is on file with the Library of Congress.

Editor's notes
This publication is intended to support personal growth and should not be thought of as a substitute for the advice of health care professionals. The author's advice and viewpoints are his own.

Alcoholics Anonymous, AA, and the Big Book are registered trademarks of Alcoholics Anonymous World Services, Inc.

Readers should be aware that websites listed in this work may have changed or disappeared between when this work was written and when it is read.

21 20 19 18 17   1 2 3 4 5 6

Cover illustration: studiostoks/Shutterstock.com
Cover design: Tom Heffron
Interior design and typesetting: Terri Kinne
Development editor: Vanessa Torrado
Production editor: Heather Silsbee

For my kids,
and yours.

In This Book

A Note from Sober Dad on Anonymity and the Use of the Name *God*

The Eleventh Tradition of Alcoholics Anonymous suggests that members refrain from using their full names "at the level of press, radio, and films." The Twelfth Tradition reminds us to "place principles before personalities" because of the important and foundational role anonymity plays for the common good.

These traditions started for a lot of reasons, as I'm sure you can well imagine. The fact is that *anonymous* is in the name of the group. Years after the founding of AA and the writing of the Traditions, anonymity remains the best way to ensure the reputation of the fellowship while at the same time enhancing the humility of its members.

For this reason, I chose to publish this work using a pseudonym. Rather than using Michael G., which has been a common style, I'm using a full pen name. Why? It maintains my anonymity, and I have personal, emotional ties to the name I chose.

Regarding the question of what term we use for our Higher Power, I'm comfortable with the term God. Not everyone is, and I respect that, so for the most part, I use the term Higher Power throughout the book. On the occasions where I do use the word *God*, please feel free to substitute any term with which you are more comfortable. The goal here is to talk about how to be the best sober dad you can be. So, use what's useful and leave the rest.

An Invitation to Fatherhood

Let's begin this meeting with a moment of . . . panic.

You're going to be a father!

Or maybe you're going to be a stepfather!

Maybe you already are a dad, and now you're a sober dad!

You!

Can you believe it?

Becoming a father is the only irrevocable decision you'll ever make. You can end a marriage, move to another state, quit your job, leave school . . . but once you become a parent, you're a parent for life. And not just for your life, but for the life, or the lives, of the children you bring into the world.

The good news is that you're not just any dad. You're a *sober* dad.

This means that you want to do things the right way.

Maybe do things differently from the way you were raised.

Maybe be the kind of father you never had, or always wished you had.

I felt the same way.

I'm the sober father of four children who ranged in age from eight to sixteen at the time of writing.

I've made most of the mistakes a father can make.

And yet, they're here and they love me.

The good news is that you don't have to be perfect to be a wonderful father. Children don't need perfection. They need consistency, but not absolute consistency.

They need love, but they'll survive those moments when you sound or act less than loving.

The good news about being a parent is that you don't have to be perfect to be great. So if you're interested in learning how to be a perfectly imperfect parent, you've come to the right place.

In fact, in the brilliant words of the great child psychologist Bruno Bettelheim, your child only needs a "good enough" parent.

So that's what you want to shoot for.

Not perfect.

But good enough.

What qualifies me to write a book imparting my *man-up messages* about being a sober dad?

First, that I'm sober. Second, that I'm a dad.

I'm being silly, although accurate. The main thing is that I do not have any professional qualifications. No initials after my name. No degrees.

Now I'm alarmed! How dare I write this book?

I'm writing it because, to me, the most important thing I've done with my life, after getting sober and getting married, is making the decision to have children.

Not just one, but four.

Two girls, two boys.

I love being a parent. It's the most humbling, humiliating, frustrating, exciting, gratifying, and rewarding thing in the world. My kids are awesome. I would rather be with them than with anyone else on earth. I cannot wait to see what they say and do next.

Even when they do not live up to my expectations, voiced or unvoiced, conscious or subconscious, I just adore them. I love the fact that my Higher Power trusts me enough to put me "in charge" of four young souls.

I think of our children as my secret weapon in the world— they are the means by which I get to counter the negativity, gloom, and even hopelessness that you see so much of today. I am a positive person, thanks to my sobriety, and I'm doing my best to raise children who will be equally positive, or more so, as adults.

I don't know what they'll do for a living, and I don't care, as long as they're happy and contributing in whatever way they see fit.

For me, as someone coming from a home afflicted by alcoholism, drug addiction, murder, and divorce, becoming a good father was not an intuitive or easy thing. Not to tell tales out of school, but I had a father who essentially vanished into a bottle of Jack Daniel's the night of his fortieth birthday, shortly after my sixteenth birthday, and we've scarcely seen him since.

By his own choice, he has seldom seen my children, even though we currently live only about four hours apart.

I don't think he thinks he's a bad grandfather or anything like that. He remarried, moved on, and you know the story.

Perhaps firsthand.

So I knew what I didn't want to be as a father.

But what did it mean to be a *sober* father?

I had no idea.

So I went on a long journey of exploration. Once we got a positive on the pregnancy test, I began reading every book on parenting I could get my hands on. I attended countless classes and seminars. I spent endless hours on the therapist's couch, assessing what went wrong, trying to figure out how to put things right.

And, of course, time passed. I look at the pictures of them from early childhood, and I can barely remember when they were small, even though it wasn't that long ago.

I do know that I've learned a ton of lessons from having to build my own model of fatherhood from the ground up.

I'm not even sure my kids would think it makes sense for me to be suggesting to other people how to be a dad, given just how many times I've lost my temper, my reason, or my sense of proportion over the years.

Or maybe they would approve. (I'm certainly not going to ask.)

Maybe—and I hope this is the case—they have forgiven me for my shortcomings and defects of character and instead see me for what I am—a man who is trying to do the best he can with the best information available.

Some of the things I've learned about being a good sober dad have nothing to do with my children.

Instead, I had to learn to resolve conflicts with my parents. I had to learn to act like an adult myself, instead of trying to get into *Guinness World Records* as the world's oldest teenager.

I had to know how to be married.

I had to know how to have a relationship with myself, for that matter.

All of these components of fatherhood are just as important as knowing how to settle a dispute, get a child to brush and floss at night, or, as they get older, set limits on an iPhone.

So this book is about being a sober father from the inside out.

Our relationships with our children don't exist in a vacuum. They take place against the backdrop of our own histories and our own abilities to handle relationships as adults.

I'm not convinced that even the best, most well-meaning therapists and other helping professionals who do not themselves come from alcoholic homes can fully understand the dilemmas we face.

Or even if our homes were themselves bastions of emotional sobriety, we alcoholics and addicts still have our own demons.

They pop up at the strangest times.

There are plenty of great books out there by professionals who have made a lifetime career of studying what it takes to be a good parent.

This isn't one of them. This is the best effort of a sober father to pass along what he has learned to other men who have made the only irrevocable decision of their lives—to become fathers themselves.

The cover of this book may have made you think it's a manual or instruction guide for raising children. Well, I tricked you. (Sorry!) If there were such a thing, it would be different for every child.

Instead, I'll highlight for you the key things I've learned, the biggest mistakes I've made, and the insights I've gained from a wide variety of sources—books, seminars, conversations with other parents, and, of course, meetings and sponsorship. The truth is, I believe the principles I've learned through working Twelve Step programs have made me a better man. A better person. So, I find myself applying a lot of what I've learned working a program to working at being a better parent.

The good news is that you can be a great father. A wonderful, loving dad whom your children will adore and look up to, and about whom they will one day say, "I had a great dad."

It's hard to be a great father without becoming a better man, so becoming a better man is actually a side benefit of parenting.

If that's what you want, you found the right book.

If you're a #DareToBeGreatDad, keep in touch with me online.

SoberDad@gmail.com
#SoberDad

"You Might Not Have Had a Happy Childhood, but You Sure Are Having a Long One"

That's what my sponsor told me one day when I was whining about something. I don't remember what I was whining about, but I sure remember what he said.

Why does it take nine months for a baby to gestate inside a woman's body?

I don't know, but I do know this: The nine months of pregnancy give the father a chance to finally grow up.

If you're fortunate enough to have that period of time ahead of you, use it wisely. We'll talk about how in this chapter. If you already are a father (sober or not) and simply want to become a better father, the ideas in this chapter pertain to you as well.

You can't still *be* a kid when you *have* a kid. That's the message of this chapter.

Sportscaster Colin Cowherd likes to talk about the guy who wears his baseball cap backward. He might make a great wingman in a club, but you don't want Backward Baseball Cap Guy to be your quarterback and the face of your franchise.

And yet, wearing your baseball cap backward is basically a sign of the times.

It's a way of saying, "I'm cool. I'm casual. I'm stylin'."

It means you're a *guy*.

Guyhood is a period of suspended adolescence in between childhood, which never seems to end (as my sponsor suggested about me), and manhood, which never seems to arrive.

Think about the males you know. Are they men? Or are they guys?

Do they wear their baseball caps backward or forward?

We have millions of role models who want to be guys: our buddies in meetings. Celebrities. People we see at the mall.

The problem is that a guy cannot raise a child.

It takes a man.

So if your wife, girlfriend, or whatever (your partner, going forward) has just informed you that she is pregnant, you've got less than nine months to grow up.

The baby's gestation will take care of itself.

It's *your* gestation that we need to think about right now.

Before you can really be present as a husband or father, it's essential to make that all-important, and all-too-often postponed, transition from guyhood to manhood. That's what I'd like to talk about with you right now.

We have some mistaken ideas in our society about what manhood really means.

If I say *manhood,* what comes to mind?

John Wayne?

Fighting?

Showing no emotion?

Seducing large numbers of women?

One mood, all the time?

That's what comes to my mind. What about you? Those are the ways in which our culture has conditioned us to think about manhood. But those really are markers of guyhood, not manhood.

So what is manhood?

I define manhood as a willingness to embrace adult responsibility. Personal responsibility.

So what does that look like?

For people like us, for starters, there's sobriety.

In case it's not clear yet, I'm a firm believer in the Twelve Steps. Without getting all touchy feely, I trace most of the growth I've made as a person during the past decades as well as my sobriety back to working and living a program.

So, again, what does embracing responsibility for my sobriety mean? If you have an issue with alcohol or substance use, it means working a program. What does it mean to have a program? Having and defending a sobriety date. Choosing and making use of one's sponsor. Carrying the message. Doing the drill. So before we even start talking about changing diapers or warming up the formula or breast milk, we've first got to start with a look in the mirror.

If there was ever a time to tighten up your program or get on board with one, this is it.

So now let's ask the key question: What do children really need?

They don't need to live in a mansion on a hill. They don't need to be chauffeured in a 7 Series. They don't need season tickets. They don't need all the things you might not have had when you were growing up.

(Incidentally, a friend of mine says that he didn't grow up by age eighteen—he just "got big." He only grew up when he got sober.)

Children need consistency, ideally from both parents.

As long as children have at least one balanced and emotionally present parent, they'll be okay. In a perfect world, they have two such parents. In your child's perfect world, one of those emotionally balanced adults . . . is you.

Everything else is gravy.

Finding out that your partner is pregnant can be and should be a sobering moment.

A recognition that life is about to make greater demands on you than ever before.

It's awfully hard to rise to the occasion when you're "in and out of the rooms," as we say in recovery.

I can't tell you what to do. I don't have that kind of moral authority over you, and that's not how Twelve Step programs work. We don't tell each other what to do. We make suggestions. As in, it's suggested that if you are jumping out of a plane, you should have a parachute on and, at the appropriate moment, pull the rip cord.

So the idea here is this: If your program is inconsistent, how will you ever be consistent as a parent?

If you aren't showing up for yourself, how will you ever show up for that helpless little person who will call you daddy?

I'm not trying to induce guilt.

I'm trying to induce reality.

One of the themes of this book is that self-care for fathers is extremely underrated. The focus is on the mother and child, as well it should be. But we men are people, too! We have emotional, physical, and sexual needs, many of which are not being met during this critical stage of life. One of the things we will discuss at length in this book is how we men can best take care of ourselves—not just while our wives or partners are pregnant or when our children are extremely young, but at every time.

Are you getting to enough meetings? Have you taken the Twelve Steps? I've seen meetings change a lot in the twenty-eight years since my first Al-Anon meeting (I've been sober for twenty-four years at the time of writing this book). Today in AA, there seems to be an unfortunate acceptance of the idea that you can just hang out in meetings for years without doing your Steps, and you're doing just fine. In reality, physical sobriety is terrific, and we all have to have it. But physical sobriety without emotional sobriety—without the reawakened spirit that recovery provides—simply isn't going to cut it when you have a child. So, what work are you doing to support both your physical and emotional sobriety, either inside or outside of a Twelve Step program?

You've heard about all those sleepless nights after the baby's born, right? It's no joke. It's a huge test of your program to have a newborn in your home. Your partner is going to be exhausted and going through all sorts of hormonal changes. You're going to be pretty cooked a lot of the time, too. You and your partner may not see eye to eye about how to be a parent—few couples automatically do. Will you have the dispute-resolution tools you need when that bell rings? Or will you revert to being the pre-sober, selfish, self-centered baseball-cap-on-backward guy you were before you stopped drinking or using?

These aren't theoretical questions. These are the realities we will face, and the smart choice is to use the nine-month stretch before the baby arrives to work on ourselves.

The Big Book, *Alcoholics Anonymous,* tells us that one who believes physical sobriety is enough is "unthinking." It's time to start thinking, and to start thinking of someone other than ourselves. If you haven't made a surrender by taking the first three Steps, if you haven't done the self-examination that the next four Steps require, if you haven't made your amends, and if you aren't taking responsibility for your actions and enlarging your spiritual life, are you really the best possible version of you?

If you need to turn your life around, to grow up and be the man your family needs you to be, then start by turning around that cap on your head. Turn your hat around, turn your life around. Plain and simple.

There's time. To quote the venerable philosopher Larry the Cable Guy, "Git-r-done."

I understand that it's hard to get to meetings sometimes. We're tired, or it's inconvenient, or whatever. In reality, if we don't get to meetings now, before the child arrives, do we really believe our calendars will suddenly open up once the child is born? If anything, this is the time to stockpile meetings, to load up on spirituality, to pack in all the AA, NA, MA, CA, and OA you can get. (Alcoholic parent or loved one? Al-Anon. Talk too much in meetings? Try OnandOn.) Seriously, even under the best of circumstances, becoming a father for the first time is incredibly stressful. You're not going to know what's flying, and if it's the first child for your partner, much of the time, neither will she.

Why is the baby crying? Is she hungry? Tired? Sick? Angry? You may have heard the expression that for an addict, getting into a relationship is like pouring Miracle-Gro on your character defects. Becoming a father, in comparison, is like pumping up your character defects with steroids. There will be times when you won't even recognize the man in the mirror. So as long as you're looking at him, maybe it's time to take that baseball cap and have it face forward.

Let's talk about money. Babies are expensive! Assuming your health insurance is in order, you still may have a great big copay when your partner gives birth. Let's pray that your child is born healthy, but sometimes situations arise and additional tests are necessary. Somebody's got to pay for it. And even if everything is perfectly fine, diapers aren't free. If your partner stops working outside the home, there's an income stream to replace. You'll need a car seat, by the way, and they aren't cheap, either.

I'm not trying to scare you, although come to think of it, maybe I am! My point is that one of the most important things you can do during your wife's pregnancy, after you've got your own AA program straightened out, is to figure out how you're going to pay for this delightful young creature about to enter your life. Maybe you've always dreamt of being an actor, a writer, or a professional athlete. I support your dreams. I encourage them. I also suggest that you put them away for the time being and instead focus on what I call CPR—something that will put *Cash in your Pocket, Right now.* Do you have a steady stream of income? If not, can you go get one? My sponsor says that he's never surprised when an addict gets sober. He is only surprised when an addict gets a job.

The funny thing about us alcoholics and addicts is that we don't want jobs—we want a position! We only want work commensurate with our exaggerated sense of self-importance! Well, it's time to grow up. In a pamphlet on the Seventh Step, Lois W., Bill's wife and the cofounder of Al-Anon family groups, defines *humility* as knowing who you are.

If you aren't a famous artist, writer, singer, or whatever right now, maybe you will become one, one day. Right now, however, it's time to bring home the Benjamins, because when a baby comes through the door, money flies out the window.

When I first got sober, my sponsor told me to get a job—any job. He called it a "sobriety job"—something you did in order to demonstrate to yourself that you actually had value to other people. When we were drinking, we didn't. Self-esteem tends to plummet. That was my situation.

I have a JD degree from Columbia Law School, one of the best and most competitive law schools in the country. By the time I got sober, seven years after graduating law school, my classmates were making partner at the top firms in the country. Me? I was on heating assistance, because I was dead broke.

So I got a job temping, for $7 an hour, because I couldn't think of anything else I was good at. The temping firm could have sent me to one of the law firms where I had briefly worked, but my Higher Power spared me that humiliation. I made that $7 an hour and I was grateful for it. Little by little I built a financial life for myself, which is a story for another day.

The main thing is this: If you aren't bringing in money now, it's time to start. You can drive for Uber. You can wait tables. If you've got a strong back, you can work for a moving company. If you can write code, write code. What you do to bring in money, as long as it's legal and ethical, doesn't even have to relate to your education, training, past employment, or lifetime goals. You just have to have a steady stream of income.

The number one thing that breaks up marriages, and as a result, families, is fighting over money. Not having any is dispiriting, and not to go old school on you, but as the man, bringing home the bacon is your job. Right now, your partner's busy enough—and she's about to get a lot busier once that baby comes. To put it simply, as I heard early on in (or more precisely, in the hallway outside) an AA meeting, "Life is like a s*!& sandwich. The more bread you have, the less s*!& you have to eat."

Any questions?

So far, we've talked about the need to start up or step up your program so that you are spiritually fit when that baby arrives. Then we talked about the financial side of life, which essentially boils down to the importance of living AA's Seventh Tradition in your personal life and in your relationship—being financially self-sufficient. Now let's turn to another vital aspect of being a parent—looking back to the relationship you have with your parents and, if necessary, straightening that out. They say there are no big deals aside from getting sober, but working out your relationship with your parents is such a big deal that it deserves its own chapter, immediately if not sooner, and that's where we turn next.

Just Because They Were Lousy Parents Doesn't Give You the Right to Be a Lousy Son

Life is all about scenes and patterns.

Subconsciously, we recreate scenes from our past until we heal them. What does that mean? It means that if we had a certain kind of conflict-ridden or frustrating situation with our parents, we will repeat that same situation with girlfriends, spouses, bosses, siblings, other drivers, or, eventually, our own children—until we recognize our patterns and heal them.

So this chapter is all about taking a look at the relationship you have with your parents, whether they are living or dead. For example, many alcoholics come from alcoholic homes, and it can be awfully hard to think of our parents without going into a state of anger, frustration, or even rage, depending on what happened in our homes. Alcoholics like to make promises buttressed by bravado, as in, "I'll never do to a kid what my parent did to me!"

Or, "With me, it'll be different!"

Uh-huh.

I'm not buying it, based on my own personal experience. The sane course for an alcoholic or addict is to recognize that anything you don't heal, you'll repeat.

One of the most shocking experiences most new parents have is when they raise their voices to a spouse, partner, or child, or when they open their mouths to speak, and they suddenly hear the voice of their father or mother.

Where did *that* come from? I never knew I had *that* in me!

Yeah, you do.

This programming is like a series of time bombs. They get detonated by things that are happening so far below the surface that we could never consciously identify them. But they're there.

So how do you stop recreating unhappy scenes from your own childhood, scenes you may not even remember? How do you get healthy with your parents?

My sisters got sober before I did, and they gave me a copy of the Big Book, a gift I found highly insulting. Me? An alcoholic? Hardly. I was the "good child," the family hero. No way was I an alcoholic.

I did hit something of a bottom, although not my lowest bottom so far, as my twenty-ninth birthday approached. I told my sisters, who had gotten sober by that point, that I would get my dad, whose alcoholism was fairly advanced by that point, to come with me to a Mets game.

They laughed.

They told me that if I intended to spend the last birthday of my twenties with my father, I would spend it in a bar.

They even named the bar.

Stubbornly, I told them that under no circumstances would I spend my birthday in a bar with my father. I would impose my will, we would go to the game, and we would have a great time.

We spent my twenty-ninth birthday in a bar.

The exact bar that my sisters had named.

My sisters suggested that I attend an Al-Anon meeting, and

a few weeks later, on August 27, 1987, I did just that. It was an Al-Anon meeting in Cambridge, Massachusetts, with an adult-child focus. I had never been to a Twelve Step meeting before, although I certainly remembered ads for Al-Anon during *The Tonight Show* with Johnny Carson when I was a teenager, nursing a big bowl of coffee ice cream at midnight (I'm in a program for coffee ice cream, too).

The meeting was revelatory. Here were forty people, all telling parts of my story. It was astonishing. Other people had been through the same sort of insanity that I had. Of course, until then, I never labeled it insanity.

I simply called it "my childhood."

There were people my age, older people, men, women. I didn't speak, because I wasn't used to speaking, or hearing, the truth. But here was the truth in all its awesome, ugly glory. I was home.

I could not even get out of bed the next day—I was so blown away by everything I had seen and heard in the meeting. I found a library book on adult children of alcoholics and spent the day in bed, if I remember correctly, just reading and being astonished. There was a label for what I had been through.

I wasn't alone.

There was hope.

I went back the next three Tuesdays and heard more tales of woe. I don't recall hearing anything about the Steps or a Higher Power in those particular meetings, but admittedly, it's been a long time. Toward the end of the fourth meeting, I put my hand up to share. I introduced myself as an adult child and explained that I identified strongly with what everyone was saying, but I didn't really feel the need to continue in the meetings. I had enough self-knowledge that I could make it on my own. Nobody seemed too particularly alarmed by my announcement, and I didn't go back to a meeting for another year and a half.

I might have had a little bit of self-knowledge, but not enough to make a difference. I got involved in yet another long-distance relationship that turned out disastrously. If the moment of disappointment over my birthday with my father had brought me to my knees, this breakup landed me on my face.

Back I went to Al-Anon.

This time, not adult-child Al-Anon, but plain old Al-Anon. I found a sponsor, went through the Twelve Steps, went to nine meetings a week because I was too depressed to do anything else, and gradually my life came back together. I was able to process a lot of the events that I had gone through with my parents in my childhood, which was very helpful.

I learned in Al-Anon to reframe my childhood. One of the most important things I learned was that my parents, particularly my father, did not wake up every morning asking himself, "What can I do to make Michael's life miserable today?"

Instead, I learned that my father, much like me today, always did the best he could based on the information he had available to him. Like me, he grew up in an alcoholic home, and like me, he did not exactly witness or experience the best ways to raise a child. I was able to accept my father,* and after a lengthy period when I had almost no contact with him, he actually stopped drinking for a while.

I met him at his condo in Florida. We spent three days talking through the bad old days, playing golf, smoking cigars, and

---

* Not to go too Al-Anon on you, but forgiveness requires judgment, which is a Divine privilege not extended to humans . . . so if I'm judging, I'm having a role reversal with my Higher Power. That's why acceptance beats forgiveness every time.

burying the hatchet. And for once, the hatchet wasn't buried in my back.

Later on, I got sober, and he went back to drinking. He had gone into therapy when he stopped, and now he stopped therapy at about the time that I got into it. So my *Brigadoon* moment with my father did not last forever. We still speak once in a while, but as I mentioned, he has had virtually no contact with my children. He remarried and moved on, as happens in life. *C'est la vie.*

With my mother, the challenges were subtler. We were always good friends and allies. I learned outside the rooms—specifically in a therapist's office—the extent to which my mother might have relied on me a little too much. I didn't get married until I was forty-one. Coincidence? We think not.

I had no idea just how deeply enmeshed emotionally my mother and I were. In Al-Anon, they talk about detachment— the ability to separate in a healthy, emotional manner from another human being. There's detachment with love, and detachment with an ax. Usually you start with the ax and then move toward detachment with love.

In my case, five years into my sobriety in Alcoholics Anonymous, my mother and I blew up at each other over some stupid, random thing. I guess it didn't say much for my program that I was ten years into Al-Anon as well as five years sober, and I still went something like eight months without speaking to my mother. Finally, we worked things out. And then one day, things went south again.

It just happened, coincidentally—don't you love those coincidences?—the day after that next blow-up, I ran into my sponsor about half an hour prior to the beginning of an AA meeting on the Santa Monica promenade. He asked me how things were.

Things are great, I told him.

Then he asked me how things were with my mother.

Not so great.

I wasn't twenty-one at the time. I was pushing forty, and I was still in an unhealthy, push-me-pull-you relationship with my mother.

Not great.

"Here's what you're going to do," my sponsor said. "You're going to make a list called *What a Good Son Does*. On that list, you'll write down things a good son does. He calls once in a while. He visits. He remembers birthdays. He sends a card or a present. He sends flowers every so often. Things like that.

"Any time you feel a moment of rage toward your mother," he concluded, "take out that list and do one thing on it."

I've got no idea where he got that advice—whether he heard it somewhere or whether he made it up. One time, years later, I complimented him on some idea he had shared with me and he said, "Ah, I didn't make that up. I stole it from Gandhi."

Whatever.

But he was my sponsor, and I did what he said. (Usually.) So I wrote the list down.

And as God is my judge, from the time I wrote that list down right up until today, almost twenty years later, I have not felt a single moment of rage toward my mother.

A bit of anger? Occasionally. At this writing, my mother is eighty years old. She has mild Alzheimer's and suffered a stroke. Her mobility is limited, but her mind is often sharp. My sisters and I take care of her. I am proud to be her son. We love each other, and the relationship is clean.

A month after I resolved matters with my mother, thanks to the *What a Good Son Does* list, I met the woman who became my wife.

Coincidence? We think not.

Here's the point—it's very hard to have a healthy relationship with another adult if I still haven't resolved my relationships with my parents. It doesn't mean I have to be all lovey-dovey with my parents, hang out with my father and his second wife, be friends with his wife's children. It doesn't mean that I have to take abuse or bad behavior from any of them. It just means that I have to accept them for who they are and let the past be the past. As my sponsor told me, "Just because your parents might have been lousy parents doesn't give you the right to be a lousy son."

And to call my parents, or anyone's parents, lousy is probably inaccurate. Is that how I really feel about the people who fed, sheltered, clothed, and educated me? They did the best they could with the information they had available at the time, and in a lot of ways, they did a great job. And now here I am, many years later, with four kids of my own—and the joke's on me. Now I see just how hard it is to do this well, and I've been sober for more than twenty-four years.

So the takeaway is this: Where are you with your parents? Are you still angry? Do you have any kind of relationship with them? Doesn't it stand to reason that if you're going to be a good father, you need to be on good terms—or at least bearable terms—with your parents? You don't have to like them. You don't even have to love them. You just have to accept them.

Another thing I found very powerful is something my sister told me: *My parents have nothing I need.* There was a time I did need them. When I was a small child, I needed them for safety and security, for nurturing, for the basic necessities of life. That's no longer true. Today, I am an adult. I make my own way in the world. I make a living. I have made a life for myself. What exactly do I need from my parents at age fifty-eight? How about . . . nothing?

What about you?

What do you think you still need from your parents?

Here's my beef with the whole "adult child" thing.

Pick one.

Adults recognize and accept the limitations of their parents.

Children cleverly disguised as adults . . . don't.

They still think that Mommy and Daddy are going to come back, that the drinking and drugging and infidelities and violence and abandonment will somehow vanish, and there will be a big hug and kiss and "I love you."

Don't shoot the messenger (thank goodness I'm anonymous!), but I've got news for you.

They aren't coming back.

Not today, not tomorrow, not ever.

So rub some dirt on it and be a man.

Not an adult still thinking like a child.

How did I get so wise?

As the expression goes, "'Figuring it out' is not an Al-Anon slogan."

I didn't figure any of this out on my own.

I found it incredibly helpful to find a great therapist who could help me come to terms with my past, and I also have found continuing involvement in the Al-Anon fellowship to be extremely rewarding.

If you've never been to Al-Anon, there's a reason why many AAs call it "the graduate program." In AA, our primary focus, of course, is on physical and emotional sobriety and the developing of a spiritual life. Anything else—money, relationships— is secondary. When you get into Al-Anon, it's all about having relationships with other people.

If you're fortunate enough to have an alcoholic relative, friend, parent, child, whatever, that's your ticket into an Al-

Anon meeting. If you don't have such a person in your life, lie and go anyway. And of course, if you're an alcoholic, you get to go to Al-Anon so you can have a relationship with yourself.

A couple of thoughts if you do go to Al-Anon: Don't be the classic sober alcoholic Ala-Snob who considers himself superior to all those wimpy, codependent Al-Anon people. Actually, they know a lot more than you do about how to conduct a healthy relationship. You're the one with the string of failed relationships. As the Big Book says in another context, see where they are right instead of just looking to criticize and complain.

The other piece of advice: Don't attend meetings with the adult-child focus. I know some readers will squawk at this, but I have found precious little recovery in adult-child meetings. As I said, when I even hear the term *adult child,* my first thought is "Make up your minds, people. You're one or the other." And that's one of the core ideas we're tackling as sober dads, right? You've decided you are a grown-up.

Of course, the meetings were extremely helpful to me when I was brand-new. Adult-child meetings tend to be focused squarely on the problem, and people whine an awful lot. Since everyone else is whining, it must be okay, right? Uh, no. Think about it: If venting about your problems made you happy, then people who vent a lot ought to be the happiest people in the world.

Of course, they're miserable, which is why they're always venting.

If adult child meetings had more of a focus on recovery, I'd still be making them part of my meeting schedule today. If you feel otherwise, great. Just one man's opinion.

Find a good Al-Anon meeting with a bunch of crusty old-timers, male or female, who have a ton to share with you about how human relationships really work. You'll be awfully glad you did.

And, finally, now that you're talking to your folks again, please tell them I said hi.

If Marriage Were Easy, Everyone Would Do It Well

I used to call my sponsor and complain about certain things going on in my marriage I didn't care for, and he would always say the same thing.

"What I'm hearing from you, I hear from all the guys I sponsor. It's not your marriage or anybody else's marriage. It's just how marriage is.

"If you don't like it, and you still want to live with somebody, your only option is to go gay." Before you get offended at that statement, keep reading.

I heard that so often that finally I decided it just wasn't worth the trouble of complaining. So I just accept what goes on as standard for marriage and let it go at that.

A few years later, I had a gay Al-Anon sponsee.

One day, he called me with the same relationship issues that I used to complain to my sponsor about.

"You blankety-blank,"* I told him. "You just took away my plan B!"

My point: Relationships are not easy. Marriage isn't easy. It's especially difficult for alcoholics, addicts, and others who didn't grow up with the proverbial white picket fence enveloping a calm, loving home. As the literature suggests, we are

---

* I used much saltier language, but this is a family book.

just guessing at what a good relationship should look like, and sometimes our expectations are way out of line with reality.

Psychologist Terry Gorski writes and speaks about the Twelve Steps and was a major influence on my early recovery. There was a particular speaker tape of his that got passed around Al-Anon when I came in,[1] clandestinely, like *samizdat* material in the former Soviet Union.* He says that the addict's concept of what a love relationship should look like is based on the only successful relationship he or she probably saw growing up—the love that the alcoholic parent had for his or her bottle.

In other words, Gorski says, addicts expect their partners and relationships to be like booze or, better still, cocaine, blowing their minds any time they want.

That's not how it works.

That's not your partner's job.

If you pull back the lens and take a broader view of marriage, it's interesting what you find. One of my favorite authors on relationships, Warren Farrell, wrote a book years ago called *Why Men Are the Way They Are.*[2] Love that book. Farrell says that a woman achieves her primary fantasy—the committed love of one man—on her wedding day, which is exactly when the man surrenders his primary fantasy—multiple sexual partners. No wonder, Farrell concludes, that relationships are a never-ending World Series between the commitment Giants—the women— and the commitment Dodgers—the men. Okay, Farrell's insights may seem a little antiquated, but how much does this line of thinking still influence our relationship dynamics?

I also once heard a sober alcoholic quote the seventeenth-century French philosopher Montesquieu from an AA podium to the effect that "people and relationships are like flies at a

---

* You can Google the reference. I'd explain it myself, but I don't have time; I'm busy writing a book about parenting.

screen door. The ones that are on the outside want to get in, and the ones that are on the inside want to get out."

Cynicism aside, John Gray, who wrote *Men Are from Mars, Women Are from Venus,*[3] says that 90 percent of people in therapy are women, and 90 percent of people in jail are men. In other words, when it comes to naming, understanding, and thinking through feelings, women have a huge advantage over us. So much so, in the unforgettable words of Dave Barry, that "a man in a relationship is like an ant on top of a truck tire."

Why? Because he doesn't know where he's going, but he does know it's not going to be an easy ride.

One thing marriage has in common with working a program is that if anybody tells you it's easy, run like hell. And relationships only get infinitely more complicated when baby makes three (or four or five or, in my case, six).

In this chapter, I'm going to share with you what I know—what little I know—about how to have a successful relationship. I'm not speaking from the perspective of a therapist or other healing professional. I'm just speaking from the perspective, for whatever it's worth, of a man who's been married sixteen going on seventeen years.

The point of this chapter is that getting your relationship with your partner as strong as it can be is just as important as getting your sobriety and your relationships with your parents squared away. It's so funny when I'm watching a movie and a couple has decided to have a baby to strengthen their relationship. Not so much. Babies may weigh less than tabby cats, but their ability to lay asunder a relationship that has taken months or years to build is unparalleled.

Let's be clear:

Babies don't strengthen relationships.

Committed relationships—dare I say marriages—exist to strengthen babies.

That is, a strong marriage or relationship is exactly what the child needs.

So this is why the time before the baby comes is the time to focus on your relationship. And there are two aspects to that process.

One is to understand how you function in relationships.

The other is what you need to work out with your partner.

My starting point is the concept that pretty much all couples go through serious challenges, and usually the same kinds of serious challenges. The couples who survive are the ones who deal with those challenges.

That's so important, I'll say it again, but in a slightly different way, to demonstrate my astonishing versatility as a writer.

Most couples who don't stay together have the exact same problems as couples who stay together.

It's just that the couples who stay together find a way to solve those problems.

I was in the drugstore the other day and noticed a *People* magazine cover explaining that, after four years, a famous movie star and her husband were giving up on their marriage. I read the article to find out what sort of problems they faced, aside from where to invest her $70 million net worth. They were up against the same things as the rest of us, just with a few more zeros to the left of the decimal point. Conflicts over careers, time, and authority. Garden-variety stuff. It just proves my point—couples who separate and couples who stay together have the same problems. It's just that the couples who stayed together worked through them.

Look, there are only so many problems a couple can have, right?

Money.

Sex.

In-laws.

Raising kids.

Communication.

Negotiating time.

Anger and other bad habits.

Um . . . that's about it.

If you can add to this list, email me at SoberDad@gmail. com. I'll acknowledge your contribution in the next edition of this book, and your divorce lawyer will make a note as well.

In other words, having a great relationship isn't purely a mixture of God's will and good luck. It takes two people reasonably mature enough to recognize that the good of the relationship outweighs anything else, and they are willing to work things out. It means running your marriage or relationship on the basis of the First Tradition—that your common welfare (not your ego or your partner's ego) comes first.

Marriage, or any committed relationship, is not an arena where one party can be unyielding and somehow get away with it. One of the themes of AA's *Twelve Steps and Twelve Traditions* is that when you have a healthy relationship with your Higher Power, you no longer need to play God to your fellows nor allow them to play God to you. When we get out of the business of playing God and trying to control other people, because we are sane enough to recognize that it's probably not that great an idea, we now have an opening for a decent relationship. So if you still have your God costume on (please don't wear it on Halloween; it'll scare the neighbors' kids) or if you're still willing to be pushed around by a strong personality, ask this question: Is this going to be healthy for you and for the children involved?

Probably not.

I'd like to offer you some thoughts on how you can get your relationship to be where it needs to be, if it isn't there yet, so that when baby makes three, the relationship still adds up.

As with everything else in sobriety, before we start thinking about other people, we have to start thinking about ourselves. We have to look at what our part is in making a relationship good or bad.

The first thing to know about a truly committed relationship—and I don't mean a Hollywood marriage, which is just an extended date with a wedding cake, paparazzi, and telephoto photos of the honeymooners topless on a Greek island—is that it's hard.

Why is the divorce rate so high? Because a lot of people give up.

Why do they give up? Everyone has an opinion. Here's mine:

A marriage with clearly defined no-exit rules, meaning that your intention is to stay and work things out, come what may, is *the arena that provides the highest level of personal growth*. To put it simply, *most people do not want to grow as much as it takes to be in a healthy union with another person*.

When it comes to relationships, most people want to take the easier, softer way, especially us alcoholics and addicts. We *love* the easier, softer way. It's our favorite thing in the world. So when we have to step up and demonstrate some maturity, oh my God. You've got to be kidding. *Moi?*

Alcoholics and addicts love to disavow responsibility for the poor quality of their relationships. Here's a line that you hear frequently in Twelve Step meetings, or a variant thereof: "I have a broke picker."

A "picker" in AA parlance is the part of you that chooses people to date (or sleep with or take hostage).

A "broke picker" means that your faculty for selecting dating partners operates poorly and keeps presenting you with the wrong kind of person.

In other words, there's nothing wrong with *me*. I just pick all the wrong people. If I just picked the *right* person for once, everything would be groovy.

What an irresponsible thing to say. When somebody says that in a meeting, five other people immediately agree, and six more roll the thought around in their heads and come to the same conclusion that they, too, have broke pickers. It's all *the other person's* fault! I have no responsibility for the fact that my relationships have generally been nasty, brutish, and short. It's always his or her fault, but never mine.

Please.

I used to say the exact same thing, that I had a broke picker, until I did a little bit of inventory on my romantic excursions. In virtually every relationship I've ever been in, I brought out the worst in my partner.

I'll say it again because it's so important: In virtually every relationship I had ever been in, prior to marriage, I brought out the absolute worst in my partner.

It's amazing how, when you lie to someone you're in a relationship with, she just isn't herself.

It's amazing how, when you're compulsively overcontrolling, the other person feels manipulated and has an urge to strike back.

Or just get the hell out of there.

I say all this because when people want to fix their relationships, typically, what they really want to do is fix their *partners*. Man, there's nothing addicts love more than a fix, right?

They operate from a position of "if only she would just . . ." and then they finish the sentence with whatever they think would make them happier. Give them more sex. Clean up the house. Make more money. Whatever. The reality is that if you aren't happy now, you ain't gonna be happier then. Any time we tie our happiness to external events or other people, we are setting ourselves up to be miserable.

One of the most foundational aspects of Twelve Step recovery is the Serenity Prayer, which was introduced to the program when someone in the AA central office in the early 1940s saw it in the newspaper and showed it to Bill W., who immediately fell in love with it. The Serenity Prayer isn't in the Big Book, but we've been saying it in meetings for seventy years, which gives it a fair amount of authenticity.

God, grant me the serenity to accept the things I cannot change—that's everybody else.

Courage to change the things I can—that's me.

And wisdom to know the difference—it shouldn't even take wisdom to know the difference between you and other people.

Here's a clue.

Other people are over there.

You're over here.

Any questions?

So if you want to have a happier, healthier relationship, there's so much you can do before you even say one word to your partner. It really all starts with what kind of person you are.

My alcoholic personality did not vanish overnight or magically transform itself into Mr. Wonderful by the time of my first AA anniversary. Instead, it's packed in grease and I can reassemble it in the dark. I don't even need to drink to be That Guy again. All I have to do is become hungry, angry, lonely, tired, or some combination thereof, which we refer to as "HALT." Professionals call HALT an age regression, meaning that you go backward in maturity until you eat/chill/connect/nap. If a sober alcoholic regresses in maturity, the results are seldom pretty. Usually he will regress or go backward to the time prior to his sobriety when he was even more immature. That would not be good.

And yet, we forgive ourselves so quickly for our own raised voices, angry gestures, withdrawal, or whatever our strategy for expressing our displeasure is. We somehow expect that the people with whom we are involved will never stoop to such lows.

This is a long way of saying (yet again, people!) that if you're going to *have* a baby, it's time to grow up and stop *being* one yourself! It's time to recognize that the quality of your relationship is, to a striking degree, in your hands. I'm not saying you have to take the lead because you're a man. I'm saying you have to take the lead because you're *you*. Your partner has the same responsibility you do. Women have to come to the relationship in a state of adult readiness. Not readiness for combat—readiness for maturity and growth. Readiness to deal with whatever happens in a sensible, sober manner. Not all the time, not perfectly. But that has to be our general rule.

My sponsor calls character defects "bad habits." I like that. When we use the term *character defect,* which, after all, Bill used in the Steps, we are letting ourselves off the hook. "I cannot possibly do any better. I have a defective character! My character came factory equipped with defects! What am I supposed to do about that? It's not my fault!"

On the other hand, if you think of anger, fear, self-pity, control, manipulation, resentment, and rage as bad habits, everything changes. I can eliminate a habit by practicing the opposite trait. Instead of manipulating, I can live and let live. Instead of trying to control outcomes, I can let people and situations be and develop as they will. Instead of anger, I can practice patience. If there are two people in a relationship, and at least one of them is working strenuously to be a better person, doesn't it stand to reason that the relationship has a much better chance?

That's why I say that there's so much you can do to improve your relationship, even before you say one word to your partner. Or even before you *find* a partner. So much of this is internal. So much of this is attitude.

This reminds me of something Dr. Terry Gorski said on that audiocassette (man, I'm old) I mentioned earlier.

He told his therapist, "I want a woman who is brilliant, happy, sexy, and financially independent."

To which his therapist replied, "What would a woman like that want with *you*?"

Ouch.

Look, Alcoholics Anonymous is a spiritual program—we're not a program with a spiritual angle. We're just flat-out spiritual. This means that we have the added benefit of not just trying to change our bad habits ourselves—we can ask for the help of our Higher Power. This is what the Seventh Step is all about. It's about saying to my Higher Power, "I want to be a better person. Please help me."

It's my experience that every time I ask for help, God meets me at least halfway. But as Chuck C. wrote, or more accurately was quoted, in *A New Pair of Glasses*,[4] an early, unofficial AA text, "God is a gentleman—he doesn't go where he isn't invited." So if I want to be a better person, not just for my own sake but for the sake of the people around me, and especially for the sake of that person who hasn't been born yet and deserves better than my worst, I need to ask God for help.

I do that on a daily basis. The Big Book, as we've discussed, says that we are "unthinking" if we believe that physical sobriety is enough. What good am I in a marriage or any committed relationship, what good am I as a father, if I am still the same jerk I was when I was drinking? Judgmental, withdrawn, emotionally unavailable. Don't I have enough bad habits to work on without having to drag my wife into it?

I was on the phone with a longtime AA friend tonight, and he was despondent over the fact that his granddaughter was suicidal and had just entered a treatment program to address her depression. Where does her depression stem from? The devastating way her father, a practicing alcoholic, treats her. There is a cost to others when we drink, and when we drink, we don't recognize the cost to others.

That's why I say that the first step in improving your relationship with your partner is to improve yourself as a human being. I'm not talking about the kind of personal improvement that comes from reading the Great Books or going to museums (although that's also recommended). I am talking about showing up and being a kind person. After all, isn't that all you really want from her?

And lots of sex, of course. I know. You're still a guy.

What if your partner wants to talk about the relationship? Sit and listen. Immediately. See if you can learn something. Notice your own discomfort, if any, but primarily see what she has to say. And then act on it. Good husbands always want to become better husbands.

This reminds me of a conversation I had—well, it was less of a conversation and more of a lecture—from my first sponsor, a couple of months after I joined AA. We were talking about dating.

Here's what he said, words that were burned into my consciousness.

"You don't know the first thing *about* women," he told me

with disgust. "All you know about women is how to try to f*** them. Just take one out for coffee and listen to her. Learn something. Try to understand what makes her tick."

Wow, I thought. He really knows me.

Then I remembered he'd only been sponsoring me for a couple of weeks, and this turned out to be his stock speech to every newcomer.

He was right, of course.

One last topic for this chapter. If you were to ask me which character defect—bad habit, that is—would be most destructive to a relationship, my answer might surprise you.

It's not anger or manipulation or even the fact that you drink milk directly out of the milk carton and then put it back in the fridge.*

It's playing the victim.

Look, everybody has a victim story. Maybe you grew up poor or in an alcoholic or violent home. Maybe someone in your family stole your inheritance or somebody at work got you fired from your dream job. Or maybe you got dumped by the girl of your dreams . . . back in third grade.

But here's the deal. Alcoholics treasure their stories of their victimhood. They relish telling them over and over, especially in meetings, and even more so in meetings where there are hot newcomer women, so they can play the "pity me, sleep with me" card.

The only problem is that victims are, well, babies on an emotional level. I'm not denying that what happened in your childhood happened. I am saying that you've got to deal with it and not let it dominate your thinking. Victims are unattractive, except to other victims. If you really want your relationship

---

* I know you. I'm watching.

to be a competition among victims, that's your choice. On the other hand, eventually she'll leave you—maybe for a wealthier or more physically attractive victim—and you'll have an even better victimhood story to tell ("She left me! For a wealthier or more physically attractive guy!"), but you'll be seeing her lawyer in court, and he'll take you for everything you have, and then you'll *really* be a victim.

So commit to working through whatever you went through and stop clinging to your victimhood story. Aside from its (debatable) usefulness in getting hot newcomer women to pity you and maybe sleep with you (shame on you for hitting on newcomers!), all it does is keep you in a state of non-adulthood, otherwise known as immaturity. Otherwise known as "not marriage material."

One side note—if you're a dad, you're probably either married or in a committed relationship. So you should be the last person on earth hitting on newcomer women, otherwise known as "thirteenth stepping." If you're doing this, man, clean up your act. Maybe you aren't getting as much sex as you want. Maybe you aren't getting as much attention at home. If you are seeking some extracurricular loving, that's your business, not mine, but for God's sake, don't use the newcomer to meet those needs.

Okay, enough of that.

So let's wrap this chapter up. I'm assuming that today you know more about women, or at least the one you've selected,* than I did when I was newly sober. I'm hoping that you buy into my argument that before you can even have a healthy relationship, there must be an emotionally healthy *you*. Remember that the mathematics of love isn't addition, as in "One person who

---

* Dude, deal with reality—*she* selected *you*.

is halfway mature plus another person who is halfway mature adds up to one healthy couple."

Nope. It's multiplication, as in, "One person who is halfway mature *times* another person who is halfway mature results in just 25 percent of a healthy relationship."

If your relationships haven't been working, *do the math.*

Okay, if seeking to reduce or eliminate your bad habits is what you work on by yourself, what exactly do you work on with your partner? That's the topic of our next chapter.

Accept That Parenthood Takes Your Relationship into Uncharted Waters

Let's talk a little more about how marriage changes when you have kids.

When I was a kid, my parents had friends we'll call the Johnsons. Mr. Johnson was a therapist, and he looked and sounded a lot like Bob Newhart on the old *Bob Newhart Show*—thinning hair, quiet demeanor. Nobody's idea of a wild man.

We took a summer vacation at the beach with his family one year, and he, my dad, and I were playing Frisbee. A dog ran by.

We all watched the dog go, and Mr. Johnson said, "Mammals love speed."

Three weeks later, he left his wife, his family, and his therapy practice for another woman. He blew out of town, leaving his whole life behind him—and in disarray.

Mammals sure do love speed.

Message: You never can tell.

I tell this story because it serves as a constant reminder to me that marriage isn't easy, especially when children are involved. Mr. Johnson was a therapist, for God's sake. If anyone should have been equipped to handle the ups and downs of family life, he should have been that person. Who knows what motivated him to make the move he made. We never saw him again, so I don't have a conclusion to the story other than the lesson I learned, which is that if marriage were easy, everybody would do it well, and forever.

I've read a gazillion parenting books over the years,* and I realize now that virtually all of them begin with the premise that the parents are happily married and basically on the same page when it comes to issues about their children. The stance of these books seems to be that you and your wife are reasonable people who get along fine and just need some specific advice about handling situations with your kids—bedtime, screen time, expectations around chores, and so on.

That's not my experience.

It may not be yours, either.

Marriage is much harder than it appears. The gloomy statistics surrounding divorce suggest that successful marriage is impossible, except for a lucky few. I'm not here to tell you if the statistics are accurate. Instead, I would like to repeat a point I made earlier in the book, and elaborate on it because it is so darned important:

Couples who stay together face the same problems as couples who divorce. The only difference is that the couples who stay together work through those problems.

In this chapter, let's take a realistic look at the nature of marriage, which is somewhat different from the rosy, optimistic sense you receive when reading all those other (although perfectly acceptable) parenting books. Dating is easy, because when the date is over, whether it's that night or the next morning, somebody goes home.

---

* Many of which I've quoted for your reading pleasure.

Marriage is hard because you're both home. You're both always home. We men like to joke that we have "one mood all the time." It's not true. Men cycle. Men get moody. Men get sarcastic. Men get difficult. Men get confrontational for no reason. In short, men do all the things that we criticize women for doing.

There's an old country song where a guy is talking to his old girlfriend about his new girlfriend, which is a little hinky, and he says, "She thinks I'm perfect and that I love her cat, but you know me better than that."

There's a world of insight behind that line. It suggests, for starters, that even though we are eternally committed to our spouses, we don't always trust them enough to share our deepest emotions with them. Sometimes we do, and we find out that they really didn't want to hear it. So we get guarded about what we say. I don't know if this is a good thing or a bad thing, but it's just reality. Men get, well, careful.

Consider the Jewish wedding custom of stepping on the glass during the marriage ceremony, which symbolizes the fact that when something is broken, and you try to put the pieces back together, it doesn't always come out the same way. That's how it is in relationships. We men sometimes feel that any statement we make—if it is not to our partner's liking—becomes etched in stone, part of the historical record. Show me a man who gives single-syllable answers, and I'll show you a man who, at one point in the past, overshared.

It's hard to have a deep, intimate relationship if you don't feel comfortable saying anything that's on your mind. Most men don't say anything that's on their mind, opting for safety over intimacy. To paraphrase Thomas Jefferson, anyone who trades safety over intimacy will one day have neither.

So intimate communication isn't always the easiest thing. Most of us men don't understand what intimacy really is. It's not just sex. Sex is a byproduct of intimacy. Intimacy is opening yourself up and revealing yourself to the other person, so they know exactly who they're dealing with, warts and all. In a perfect world, your partner will accept you and not mark you down because of your shortcomings. Of course, we don't live in a perfect world.

So part of early marriage is finding out what you can and cannot say, where the lines are, what your partner's comfort zone is for intimate conversation. In many cases, sober dads are people who picked out their spouses, or were picked out as spouses, back when they were still drinking. So the marriage has a history, and not always a happy one.

There may be some lingering element of mistrust on the part of a wife who has been married to a practicing addict or alcoholic, and it would be hard to blame her. A man may become resentful of the fact that his wife's continued love and affection for him is dependent on his continued sobriety, but we might as well get used to it. If I ever drink again, and I hope I don't, my wife will love me. She'll miss me, and she'll probably still love me, but that love will be from afar.

All those books about child rearing fail to mention the fact that a woman may fall into a postpartum depression immediately after the birth of the child. She may also have a delayed reaction, and the postpartum depression begins after she stops breastfeeding or just some point down the line.

The buildup to having a baby is enormous, and in your own romantic way, you more likely than not contributed to that pre-baby fervor. Everybody loves to talk to pregnant women. Other women give them tips and express solidarity. Men give up their seat on the subway or bus (or should). You can play the pregnancy card at a crowded restaurant on a Saturday night and get a table quickly if you're showing enough.

Then you have the baby, and nobody wants to hear from you. All that excitement and connection with other people that your partner had when she was pregnant can vanish, now that she is exhausted, isolated, and perhaps even feeling guilt-ridden that she doesn't love motherhood, and her baby, more.

You've wandered into some pretty complicated territory, fella.

Loving a depressed person is hard. Communication dwindles to zero. Sex is a memory. You sit there and say to yourself, "This isn't what I bargained for."

They didn't warn you, did they?

Well, that's why Uncle Mikey's here, the Sober Dad himself, to give you the truth. I don't know the statistics, but I know that a lot of women go through intense depression after their first child is born, and sometimes after every child is born. Most of the time, they pull out of it. Sometimes they don't. It is vital for you to find a way not to take her depression personally, if this is what's happening in your home.

Loving someone means accepting that person as she is, where she is. Most people simply don't want to do this. They want life on their terms, not on life's terms. Marriage on marriage's terms means that if your wife goes through depression, it's up to you to continue to love her and meet her needs as best you can.

The two most destructive words in a relationship are not "F. U." or even "I'm leaving." You can always apologize or come back. The most destructive two words are the ones we say to ourselves and not to our partner, and they are, "Where's mine?"

When there is a baby in the house, and you're looking for "mine," you'll be looking for a long time. It's just not there now. It will come back if you are patient. Probably. But don't get your hopes up that something you do or say in the short term will shift the relationship such that you can somehow jolly her out of her depression. You didn't bring it on, and trust me—you cannot take it away, as much as you love your wife, or even simply out of a selfish motivation to get back a little of what you married for—love, affection, and attention from your partner.

Let's talk for a moment now about cheating.

I've never cheated on my wife, although I've certainly thought about it. As the expression goes, you can look at the menu, but you just cannot order. It's hard to understand what good could come from having a sexual relationship outside the marriage. The last time I checked, there were still sexually transmitted diseases out there, and bringing one home is probably not the gift your wife was hoping for.

On top of that, the real issue, if we delve deeply, isn't about sex—it's about emotional availability. A woman who has just had a baby does not have the same level of emotional availability that she did in prior phases of the relationship. This is not something that alcoholic men can accept graciously. The phrase "his majesty, the baby" was coined to describe us, after all.

Remember also that our default-mode thinking about relationships is what Terry Gorski says—we expect our partners to be like cocaine, blowing our minds on demand. Now, we can be as demanding as we want to be, but that does not translate into a woman who has the time, energy, or even interest in focusing on us and our emotional needs.

I have had women friends over the course of my marriage, people I have talked things over with, but that's about as far as things have gone. Am I suggesting that you have an emotional affair with another woman? One that is nonphysical but deeply connected on an emotional level? I am not. If it's the kind of conversation that you wouldn't have with your wife present, it's probably best not to have that kind of conversation with your wife absent, either. If you are going to be bold enough to conduct any kind of extramarital relationship, physical or strictly platonic, don't be stupid enough to put anything into a text or email that you may regret having read to you either in the bedroom or one day in court.

When I was fairly new in sobriety, there was a middle-aged man in our group who had been caught in the midst of an extramarital relationship, and he shared with the group his chagrin about pushing a cart in a big box home improvement store, stocking up on a mop, detergent, laundry soap, and all the other things he would now need as a suddenly single man. For whatever reason, that image has always haunted me.

The idea of dejectedly pushing a cart through Target or Wal-Mart, a mop sticking up through the chain metal, looking obvious to the other shoppers that I had been booted out of my own home, was just too dispiriting. That image, all by itself, may have kept me on the straight and narrow during these nearly seventeen years of marriage.

What else can go wrong? The two of you may have shockingly different ideas about how to raise kids. It's really interesting how little the dating process prepares us for parenthood.

In a typical job interview, you are asked to explain the nature of your experience that relates to the job for which you are being hired.

When you get married and have children, your jobs are endless. As a parent, you are running a dormitory, a restaurant and all-night snack bar, a motor pool, a wardrobe department, an entertainment center, a carpool service, a bank, and a dozen other valuable services, all under one roof.

When you are dating, the only thing that really seems to matter is whether the person with whom you are entertaining spending the rest of your life likes romantic walks on the beach at sunset, candlelight dinners in Italian restaurants, and all the sex you can talk her into.

In other words, there's a big disconnect between the things that dating people evaluate each other on and the things that parents actually have to do. In fact, there is virtually no connection between the two phases of life, except for the fact that you are screening for loving-kindness, the one trait that applies to both phases.

It may well turn out that your upbringing is radically different from your partner's. As a result, the two of you may have radically different ideas about how to raise a child. About the nature and duration of punishments. About what happens on a Sunday morning. About what chores must be performed at what age, and for what financial reward, if any. And so on and so forth until backward reels the mind.

One of the primary responsibilities early in marriage is to resolve the rules differences that partners unconsciously bring to this new relationship. If you don't think you have a lot of rules when it comes to life, it might be that you just aren't *aware* of your rules, behavior standards, or boundaries. Just wait until you have a kid.

You will suddenly discover that you have, or will instantly develop, hundreds of rules, rules to cover every minute of the day, rules to cover every situation that could possibly arise, now or in the future. Is there a possibility that some of your rules will be different from the rules by which your spouse or partner expects to manage the kids? Undoubtedly.

This is especially true because sometimes, as the expression goes, opposites attract. Part of the attraction for you might be the fact that she reminds you in no way of the home in which you grew up. Sometimes we gravitate toward our opposites; sometimes to what reminds us of our own upbringing. Opposites may be very enticing, but it means that you will simply have more rule disputes to work through, on the fly, as you go through the kaleidoscopic, ever-changing process of raising children.

The hope here is that you will not allow the process of determining whose rule to follow, or how to compromise between two conflicting rules, to keep the two of you from continuing to stand each other's company. You can win every battle and still lose the war. The healthier approach is to avoid seeing the whole thing as war and instead recognize that you and your wife are on the same team.

Keep in mind that you are playing a long game, and that at some point, you will no longer have the challenge of very small children, or the challenge of adolescence, or the challenge of teenagers. Yes, at some point you will be empty nesters, wondering where all the time went, with nothing but a bunch of photo albums, and some old report cards to show for what you've been through. Just as you have been setting up your daughter for the next man, this is the time, when your children are still in the house, when you want to set the terms for what your marriage, post-child-rearing, will be like. Don't get discouraged. Again, if it were easy, everybody would do it well.

The reality is that if fights with your spouse are still happening, it means that you're still fighting, and you should have stopped long ago. Discussing? Sharing feelings? Working things out? Yes, definitely. But the AA literature tells us that we stopped fighting everyone and everything—"We had to!"

Those aren't empty words. If you're fighting, it means that either you are letting your spouse drag you to the hole (see chapter 5), or you are dragging her to the hole, or somebody is dragging somebody. Maybe your kids are smart enough to manipulate you and are driving both of you to distraction (but not, I hope, to drink).

So now what?

The arguments may have become so frequent, and so painful, that the idea has crossed your mind to divorce.

Would that it were so simple. If you are married and with children, the word *divorce* is a bit of a misnomer. It's not as though you can call a lawyer who will snap his fingers, and the two of you never have to have any contact again. We all know stories of couples who are still fighting years after initially filing for divorce. I remember one time when I was working for a law firm—I was a lawyer long ago—that I picked up that day's copy of the state's law journal—I must have been seriously bored—only to find the latest disposition of a case involving the parents of the kid who lived two doors down from me when I was growing up.

His parents had gotten divorced eleven years prior to that newspaper article, and yet, there they were, still battling it out for whatever assets they might have had that had not gone to the lawyers for legal fees. So the whole idea of divorce as a means for getting rid of somebody is fallacious. It's just not how the world works.

Don't buy into the idea that you and your spouse can have an amicable divorce. *Amicable divorce* is up there with *partially blocked punt, a little bit pregnant,* and *military intelligence* as words that have no business being together. You guys think that you can split on amicable terms, but one of you is going to hire a lawyer, and once that happens, all that amicable stuff goes flying out the window. One of my clients in my day job, when I'm not being Sober Dad, told me this weekend that his divorce is taking about 20 percent of his time, as he answers query after query from his wife's attorney.

"It only costs her $200 to ask me a question," he said sadly. "It costs me $2,000 to put a response together, not to mention the amount of time that it takes from my work, which means that I make less money, because I'm too busy responding to her questions about how particular expenses on my credit card were handled for tax purposes." In other words, don't think there's anything simple and easy about getting divorced, especially if you have kids. Not only is it expensive, but it's incredibly time consuming.

On top of that, many alcoholics and addicts believe that if only they could get rid of the person they're with right now, they could find someone better, and then they could have a happier life with that person. It sounds great in theory, especially for alcoholics and addicts, about whom, as my sponsor said, "We can be standing at the marriage altar, about to say I do, and then we look out into the audience and there, in row two, is The One we should have married."

Let me ask you a question. How many fabulous women, and I'm talking about real women—not the ones who are inflatable or turn into a beer and pizza at midnight—how many *real* women really want to get involved with a man who has just divorced the wife who mothered his young children?

Where are you going to get the money to squire her in style? How are you going to pay for the life you live with Ms. Perfect while you're still paying off alimony and child support to Ms. Take? In short, bucko, have you really thought this whole strategy through?

Then on top of that, you do have kids. I know this is going to sound like a truly wild idea, one that comes from the dark ages of child rearing. But it really is best for your children if you guys don't divorce. If you're fighting, *just stop fighting*. If your wife is the one with the anger problem, develop a strategy for dealing with her anger. Leave the room. Keep a backpack in your car, and if she acts out, go to a hotel for the night and don't tell her where you are. Sometimes spouses, just like little kids, want to test their partners' limits. It's not just women who do this—men do, too.

Maybe she just wants to see how much you will take, to know that you will not abandon her, if abandonment is her issue. All I'm saying is that there are other ways to handle disputes than packing it in. I have yet to see any research that says that kids are better off growing up in a single-parent household or in a blended family than they are when the two parents stick together and stick it out.

Maybe unhappiness in marriage has to do with our expectations of what marriage should be. Maybe we think it's what the 1960s song says: "Goin' to the chapel and we're gonna get married . . . and we'll never be lonely anymore."

Yes, you will be lonely. You will be lonely when she is too exhausted, because of the young children or the older children, to meet every one of your innumerable emotional needs. We alcoholic men think we're John Wayne. In reality, we are wimpy and emotional. We are often the chick in the relationship, and we've married someone strong to provide us the emotional anchoring we lack. I'm not saying I did that, and I'm not saying you did that. I am saying that the dynamics of marriage are much more complex than "and we'll never be lonely anymore." If our expectations are in line with reality, then maybe we will have a higher tolerance for those moments when things aren't going exactly our way.

I'm a huge Tony Robbins guy. I love all of his audios and videos. I've been to his events. And I have in mind that there's a Tony Robbins lifestyle, where you look great, you're eating perfectly, your work is going fantastically, your savings and investments are making you rich while you sleep, your relationship is mind-blowing, and you and your main squeeze are copulating around the clock like minks.

Now reconcile that image of the perfect life with dishes in the sink that are becoming encrusted with age, the pervasive smell of dirty diapers that no disinfectant can remove, the twenty extra pounds you've put on—or is it thirty?—and the fact that you would have a six-figure balance sheet if only you could count the two figures that are to the right of the decimal point.

In other words, young people today (and maybe older ones too!) have radically inflated expectations about the way everything should be, marriage above all. After all, wasn't it magnanimous of us to get married? We who were the world's greatest Don Juans, who went through women like water, and finally deigned to commit to marriage? Where's our reward for acting so nobly? To keep it simple, as they say in the rooms, acceptance isn't getting what you want—it's wanting what you get.

If you can keep your expectations in line with reality, and if you can be the adult in the room by keeping a level head and just loving the person you're with, no matter what she's going through, you have a shot at a decent relationship. If you're aiming for a great marriage, that's fine—but your timing is lousy. Her focus isn't on you, nor should it be. She is the mother of children. You participated, but they were created inside her. Her connection to them is deeper than yours could ever be, unless she just has no regard for what she's created, and I highly doubt that's the case.

So what's a sober dad to do? Never use the *divorce* word with your wife. Never threaten it. And try as hard as you can to not even think about it. I haven't met too many long-term couples who claim that they never had a rough patch. Children take a toll on every relationship—they bring out the extreme nature of our personalities due to fatigue, fear, untreated aspects of our own pasts, and God knows what else. It's not your job to reason why. It's just your job to accept and love the person you chose.

Whenever I struggled with my relationship, my sponsor would offer me the same advice—to read the paragraphs that follow the acceptance paragraph in Dr. Paul's story on page 417 of the Big Book (or for those of you who are old school, page 449). In those paragraphs, Dr. Paul writes that whatever aspect of his wife he paid attention to grew in his "magnifying mind." If he paid attention to his wife's shortcomings, they would loom larger and larger until they were all he could see. If he paid attention to her positive traits, then all he would see would be her positives.

In short, you have a choice. You can be mature and philosophical or immature and miserable. If there's a third option, I'm not aware of it. The question is not what's wrong with this picture? The question is, now that she and the child are in the picture, what kind of man do you want to be?

Your wife and your child, or children, are waiting for your answer.

There Is a Playbook for Fighting with Your Wife

Fooled you.

I'm not going to teach you how to fight with your wife, for three reasons.

Reason number one: If you win, you lose.

Reason number two: If you tie, you lose.

Reason number three: If you lose, you lose.

Any questions?

In the previous chapter, I suggested (and we all know what "suggested" means*) that having a good relationship begins with being a good person—that is, an individual who seeks to rise beyond the character limitations that alcoholism imposes on us. Someone who strives to do the right thing and say the right thing, and then, as we say in Step Ten, when we are wrong, promptly admit it. So if the first part of a successful relationship means being the right person, the second half has to do with how we get along with our partner. And that's the subject of this chapter.

Before getting sober, and often in early sobriety, addicts don't look for partners. Instead, we take hostages. Love may

---

* As in, "If you're parachuting, it is *suggested* that you pull the ripcord on your parachute." And when do you pull the rip cord? When the people look like ants, it's too soon, and when the ants look like people, it's too late.

or may not follow. Stockholm syndrome is named for an actual event when a bank robber held several women captive in a vault and they fell in love with him, or at least they thought they did, because they subconsciously realized that their safety and chances of survival depended strictly on how the bank robber felt about them. So whenever you hear people talking about falling in love with their captors, it all goes back to the Stockholm syndrome.

Now, you're sober and presumably you've decided to begin your relationship in a healthier manner than hostage taking. This reminds me of what a jovial dinner speaker once told a Southern California AA convention, circa 1992 (when your humble author was very newly sober): "My son did everything backward. First he proposed to his girlfriend, and then he got her pregnant."*

I'm not here to judge, so however your relationship started, I'm happy for you. I don't even know why I forgot to send the two of you a wedding present. Maybe because I wasn't invited. But here the two of you are, baby's about to make three, and so the question arises: What do you owe your partner in this relationship?

The short answer is everything, fella, because I'd like to see you carry your own child.

There will come a time when you're so tired you won't even want to get off the couch to change a diaper or warm up the baby's milk, so let's see you give up your body for nine months to a small person you've never met. Let's see you become willing to put on a ton of weight, feel unattractive, go through all sorts of hormonal changes, experience morning sickness, and then

---

* He also said, "They tell newcomers not to have sex for the first year of their sobriety, but if an alcoholic goes a year without sex, he'll forget who ties up who."

face like a champion the day when you head to the hospital and deliver.*

Any takers, guys?

Waiting . . .

In other words, your partner is giving you a gift that you could not possibly repay, even if you dumped the contents of Tiffany's on your living-room floor, even if you gave her a foot massage and a new mink coat every day for the next seventy years. There is literally nothing a man can do that will compare to the acts of selflessness that pregnancy and childbirth require. I've seen my wife go through three successful pregnancies and two others that weren't. I've never been in the military, and I understand that men perform great acts of valor in the heat of battle. Nevertheless, I'll stack up what my wife has been through with the most highly decorated soldier you can find.

And they don't even give medals for breastfeeding.

Make your starting point the realization that all you had to do to become a parent was to get a woman to have unprotected sex with you.

Now compare *that* to what lies in store for her. You'll recognize very quickly that what she's going to do for you and the child who will likely bear your name makes what you are called upon to do for her look like peanuts. If you make this your starting point, you're far more likely to be approaching things in an accurate manner. Ask not what your partner can do for you. Ask what you can do for your partner.

I don't mean that in a theoretical sense. I mean go do that right this minute. I'll wait. See what she needs right now.

---

* I once asked a woman friend of mine, who has six kids, what it's like to give birth. She said, "It's like [defecating] a basketball." I think I'll stick with being a guy.

Back so soon?

Come on, big guy. Do it. I've got time.

Sometimes you hear people say that relationships are a fifty-fifty proposition with everyone giving fifty. Unfortunately, that approach doesn't work. You could be giving fifty, but if you do, you'll probably find yourself saying, "Where's the other fifty? I'm giving, but I'm not getting. I'm giving my fifty. Why isn't she?"

Once you start measuring your contribution against the other person's, it's not long before you reach the conclusion that you're doing everything and she's doing nothing. So take this whole fifty-fifty notion and junk it.

Instead, think of marriage as a 100 to zero proposition, where you give 100 percent and you expect nothing.

If you're giving 100 percent and you're expecting nothing, it's amazing what comes back to you. People *notice* when their spouses or partners make an effort. Chances are, this isn't the first relationship your partner has ever been in. She does have a basis of comparison, whether it's how her father treated her mother or how her ex-boyfriends treated her. Of course, they are exes for a reason, and you'd like to think that you're the man she chose because you treat her right and not simply because she's tired of dating.* Very simply, when you take a "give 100 percent, expect zero percent" attitude, and you *really, really, really don't keep score,* it's amazing how smoothly things can go.

My sponsor likes to say that relationships are like the song "Row, Row, Row Your Boat." It's row, row, row *your* boat, not your partner's boat. And it's gently down the stream, not madly against the current. How do you do it? Merrily. Why? Because life is but a dream.

---

* Or unexpectedly pregnant.

Next let's talk about how you talk with your wife.

If she's pregnant, or dealing with a child under two (I mean your kid, not you), the best suggestion I can offer you is this: Don't be too funny right now. Your sense of humor and hers may be radically different. She might even have married you, or at least gone to bed with you, because she liked your sense of humor. But I guarantee you that she doesn't like that same sense of humor when it's applied to *her*.

Women are especially sensitive about their bodies during pregnancy. They're afraid they won't be sexually attractive to you (or the next guy). They're afraid that you won't love them anymore, or that you'll run off with someone else. They may not feel like having sex quite as often as they have in the past, or as often as you still want it. Or you may not want that much sex, knowing that there's a little person in there. (It does weird some men out.*)

So for God's sake, don't say anything that could be interpreted as hurtful, and if you think it's possibly offensive, just don't say it. The Al-Anon book *One Day at a Time* points out that the word *sarcasm* comes from an ancient Greek word meaning "to tear flesh." Don't tear hers. And for God's sake, don't be sarcastic with your children—teens don't really understand the humor in sarcastic remarks, and then they end up just tormenting themselves, their siblings, and their schoolmates with the same sarcastic words and tonality that you aimed at them.

Back to your wife and that fight you were about to have.

If you're going to fight, fight fair. What does fair fighting mean?

---

* It weirded me out. Um, am I oversharing?

It's different for every couple, and it's worth actually having a conversation with your wife about what rules you'll fight by. Those rules might include not leaving the room, not going to bed angry,* or whatever works for you.

Here's what's worked for us.

If something's upsetting you, don't "kitchen sink"—don't make it about all the grievances you have against her, however numerous they may be. (If you have that many grievances, shouldn't you be writing a little inventory and calling your sponsor?)

Remember that the word *you* is like a loaded gun. Nothing good happens when you point the word at someone. Instead of "You do this," or, worse, "You *always* do this," say, "When X happens, I feel . . ."

In other words, don't make it about the other person's behavior. She can (and probably will) point to ten things you do that are even worse. Instead, when you make it about your feelings, no one can argue with that. She might tell you not to feel that way, or "too bad, so sad," but clearly she's a decent sort—after all, she married *you*—so it's not like that will happen all the time.

Don't wait for verbal apologies. My sponsor says that if your wife makes you breakfast the next morning, *that's* your apology.

Don't raise your voice if you can avoid it. Keep in mind that most arguments, after the first two exchanges of anger, information, or whatever, stop being about whatever the subject was and instead devolve into debates over "how dare you talk to me that way."

The next time you have an argument, see if I'm wrong. I learned this fact, incidentally, from a book on relationships

---

* As my friend Paul says, "Never go to bed angry? In that case, I wouldn't have been able to sleep since 2006."

written by . . . wait for it . . . a divorce lawyer. They know a little bit about how couples fight.

Never, ever threaten that you will divorce her or leave. Abandoning your partner when she's pregnant or with a newborn? There may be lower forms of behavior than that, but I am hard pressed to name any of them right now. Never even mention the D-word. It's all too easy for the other person to say, "You want a divorce? Okay. We'll get a divorce." And then the thing starts running of its own energy. Toss in a lawyer or two, and your marriage is gone, baby, gone.

As I've mentioned earlier, at a Jewish wedding, the groom, or sometimes the groom and the bride, step on a glass wrapped in a cloth. It's a symbolic recollection of the destruction of the Temple in Jerusalem 2,000 years ago. A secondary meaning: You can always apologize when you say something mean or inappropriate to your spouse. But just like trying to glue pieces of a glass back together after it's been broken, it never all comes back together exactly the right way.

So if you're angry, try to keep your mouth shut. One of my mentors in AA used to quote Benjamin Franklin, who said that when you're upset, count to ten, and when you're very upset, count to a hundred.

By the way, the expression "I'm angry at you" is stupid. Can you say, "I'm hungry at you"? Or "I'm horny at you"? No. You're angry, you're hungry, you're horny, you're whatever you are. But you can't be angry "at" somebody. All you can be is angry, and whoever is unfortunate enough to be in your way is going to have a bad day.

Unless you learn self-control—what *One Day at a Time* and Al-Anon so beautifully call "the lovely adventure of shrugging off hurts."

Watch your inner dialogue as well. If you call your wife (in the quiet precincts of your brain) bad names, that's how you will think of her. Even if those words don't slip out, they will color the way you see her.

She is not a bitch (or worse).

She is a human being.

And to a degree that you will never understand, her self-concept is deeply affected by how you feel about her.

So watch your language in your dialogue with her, and watch your language in your inner dialogue as you think about her.

I don't know about you, but I don't like fighting. I grew up in a home where my parents fought nightly, and loudly. It was the most dispiriting thing in the world to go up to my room, which was on the top floor, while passing my parents' bedroom, where they were yelling away. I can still not just hear but *feel* the deep bass rumble of my father's voice and the high-pitched upset in my mother's. I don't really like arguing. It's just not a good habit to get into.

As long as we're talking about disputes, let me introduce you to the concept of "the hole."

I learned this concept from another writer about relationships named John Grey. It's not the one who wrote *Men Are from Mars*—it just so happens that there's a second expert in the same field with the same name. You can find this John Grey at healingcouplesretreats.com, and you can read his book about relationships called *Relationship Tools for Positive Change*.[5] Or you can just simply trust that I'm accurately summarizing one of his key concepts here.

The idea with the hole is this: When you get seriously upset with another person, *you're no longer yourself.* On a chemical level, you're a different person from who you are when you're not angry. When you are chemicalized in this manner, you're not going to say anything that will make your relationship stronger, and there's a very high likelihood that you're going to say something that will make things worse.

Your goal with regard to the hole is to stay out of it. At the same time, you must make a commitment to yourself not to drag your partner into it, or to let her drag you into it.

The hole is where you go when a chemical change has occurred in your body so that you are operating out of the fight, flight, or freeze mentality. To put it simply, you are definitely not in your right mind.

If you feel that you are going to the metaphorical hole, get out of the room. Just walk away. You are better off. They cannot hang you for what you're thinking, but they sure can hang you for what you say. I cannot prove this to you, but experience—mine and that of other men I've spoken to—suggests that women have a much longer memory when it comes to angry or inappropriate statements made by men. In other words, it may be easy for you, as a guy, to forgive and forget what she says to you. You can just blow it off, especially the next time you have sex and operate with the little brain instead of the big brain. But it's often very, very hard for a woman to do the same thing when anyone speaks cruelly to her.

Of course, there is a lot of overlap between the chemical change we experience when we go into the hole and the chemical change we experience when we drink or take drugs. The hole is the hole is the hole. Again, we didn't spend all this time getting clean and sober to "get high" on righteous anger, or on reacting to the anger of someone else.

That's another way of saying that anything that you say in a relationship can get etched into stone. Why is this? It's because *memories are more vivid when they are bathed in emotion.* Your wife is not going to notice the ten times you take out the garbage (in my home, I joke that my responsibilities amount to cash flow and trash flow). There's no *emotion* involved with somebody taking out the garbage. So you don't get any points for that. On the other hand, if you yell at your partner, and especially if you yell at your *pregnant* partner (you bastard!), she will remember this for a long, long time. And she will *remain* distressed. That's because the experience of being yelled at is bathed in emotions—yours and hers.*

If you don't go into the hole, you won't say something you'll regret. If you don't say something you'll regret, you'll have a happier day.

Am I going too fast for you?

The bottom line is that, when your wife or partner is going through pregnancy, she's going to need more of you, and she will be less available to you. The best advice I can offer is to be philosophical. British author Simon Barnes writes that the ultimate purpose of mankind is to become an ancestor. If that's the goal, then the good news is that you're on your way. So be gentle and loving. You and I will never understand from the inside what she's going through. Don't use your partner's gradual or sudden lack of availability or focus on you as an excuse to fall back into selfish behavior patterns of the past. It's time to be a *mensch*.

In sum, take care of your program. Take care of your relationships with your parents. Take care of your relationship with yourself and with your partner.

Now let's say that you've read all this stuff and you're saying, "Yeah, but my relationship is so bad that I want to get a divorce."

If you're really thinking about divorce, consider the following.

---

* Not to compound your guilt, but the baby is listening, too.

The real issue is whether you can be as good a father from outside the home as you can from inside. Addicts are so used to examining our lives in terms of "Does this make me happy?" that it's hard for us to look at life through any other prism. If you've got young children, or a child *in utero,** this is the time when you have to sublimate your own happiness, if need be, and ask yourself instead, "What's the best thing that I can do for my kids?"

Your relationship will not be a party all the time. That's not reality. Maybe you've done all the Al-Anon and therapy a man can do, and you truly aren't making things worse. Maybe it really is all her fault. (But we both know that's not entirely possible.) The reality is that your happiness is secondary right now. *What matters first is the welfare of those children.* If you've determined that you cannot be as good a father outside the home as you can while still living with the mother of your children, then your decision is made for you.

I had an aunt who passed away from lung and lymphatic cancer in her early forties. She was on her third marriage; her first husband was an alcoholic, and her second was physically abusive. The third husband was a phenomenal human being, a true stand-up guy. Sadly, this was the second wife he would lose to cancer, which meant that he went through the entire process of watching a spouse go through treatments at times more painful than the disease itself and wither away from the brutal disease.

On one of my last visits to my aunt, I caught a ride with her husband back to the train station in Connecticut near where they lived.

---

* If you're from Passaic, this means "Your wife is pregnant."

"Everybody's concerned about Susan," I said. "But how are you doing?"

There was a long pause as my uncle stared through the front window, and I can still see the trees on either side of the country road that led to the station.

At length, he answered.

"Michael, for me, there will be another day."

And that's exactly what happened. He met and married a third woman, and they have enjoyed twenty-five years (and counting) of an outstanding marriage since that time.

So if you're in a situation that is truly failing, and if you've made the effort to get every kind of help available, whether your partner is participating in that help or not, think of my uncle. What he said was as true for himself as it will be for you: For you, there will be another day.

For most men, it's a lot easier to be the kind of father we want to be while we are still in the home. The trick is to avoid the unnecessary arguments and bickering that, when children do it, we appropriately call "childish." Be the stand-up guy God meant you to be. As the Al-Anon Do's and Don'ts say, find recreation and hobbies. Go to the gym and set a goal, like running a half marathon or doing a triathlon. Become a superstar at work. Take a painting class or join an improv comedy group.

Do something that gets you out of your head, out of your problem, and out of your home one night a week. Stock up on meetings like they're going out of style. And then be the best husband and father you can be, regardless of what is going on in your home.

Your children are watching—or will be. And they have long memories, too. Even what they don't remember consciously somehow gets encoded into the way they look at life and themselves. They're counting on you. For you, there will be another day, but this is their time, so give them all you've got.

Now, if you want your relationship to be even better, read the next chapter.

Figure Out Where She Ends and Where You Begin

Healthy boundaries are the key to happy relationships. Fortunately, there's a lot to learn from the Al-Anon fellowship about what healthy boundaries are and how to achieve them.

First, though, let's get psychological.

Frequently, you hear words derived from the field of psychology kicked around in Twelve Step meetings. Members use these terms sometimes accurately, sometimes not. One of the terms that pops up a lot, especially in Al-Anon meetings, is *codependent.* Let's pause for a moment and take a look at what *codependent,* and related terms, really means.

At the risk of oversimplifying* Erik Erikson's seven stages of human development into just four, when it comes to understanding the phases of life, this is what gets me through the night. Ready?

Developmental psychology is a fancy way of saying that there are four phases that people go through at various times in their lives. The first is codependence, which is the state of the newborn baby, who is unable to tell where he ends and where the mother begins. In the codependent phase of new life, there is an oceanic pull for the baby toward the mother and vice versa. This is one of nature's tools for ensuring survival.

---

* Perhaps because I don't know the material in a deeper manner.

After a few months, the relationship between mother and infant moves into a new phase—interdependence. This is where the baby recognizes that the mother is a different person from him, and they tend to get along just fine after this shocking realization has been made.

(How did psychologists figure this stuff out? Did they interview babies?)

The third phase is called counter-dependence, known to parents of young children as the "terrible twos." In the counter-dependent phase, the young person, somewhere between the ages of one and three, begins to get a sense of his own power and expresses that power by saying no.

The funny thing is that half the time, they're actually happy to do whatever the parent suggests. They're just *saying* no. This has nothing to do with Nancy Reagan in the 1980s.* They're just saying no because no is what two-year-olds say. Sometimes they really dig in and mean it, but most often, they're discovering the power they have and exercising it, in a rather charming manner (charming if it's somebody else's kid saying no; if it's yours, it's a nightmare). Either way, saying no is the hallmark of this third phase.

Finally comes the fourth phase, independence. This is marked by the young person, now a little bit older and perhaps a little bit wiser, saying, "I can do it myself."

Remarkably, this pattern repeats itself several times over the course of childhood, most notably in the teenage years. An adolescent is basically codependent with the parents—going along. If you ask an eleven-year-old a question, and the question has anything to do with authority or limits, the answer will not be

---

* I met a girl once around 1988 when I was on a ski trip. She paraphrased Nancy Reagan in this manner: "Just *say* no." Perfect.

about what he thinks. The answer will be about what his parents think. That's codependence. Then comes interdependence, where the young teen begins to desire some sense of separation from parental constraints. This is when many children go from saying Daddy to saying Dad. We're trying to be very mature over here.

Then comes counter-dependence, otherwise known as the teenage years, a restatement, if you will, of the terrible twos. Here, the parents are idiots and the young person only wants to take cues from his hoodlum friends.

This is extremely tough on the parents, who believe they know best and that their son's hoodlum friends know nothing. Eventually, roughly in his twenties, this oppositional mentality fades, and the parents and their adult son or daughter become friends.

One hopes.

This is independence.

I mention all this because love relationships follow these same four stages. The first stage is the codependent stage. You meet the person and *oh my God*. It's the person you've always dreamt of. No one in the world could possibly understand the instant and deep bond between the two of you. You're up all night on the phone talking. Everything is interesting, as long as it relates to the other person. The rest of your life tastes like sawdust, and you want to get home from work or school as quickly as you can just so that you can be with your immortal beloved once again.

It's just like when you were a newborn, remember?

Of course you don't remember, but that's what's happening. You are reenacting that oceanic sense of deep connection between yourself and Mom. This is nature's way of getting relationships off on the right foot. It's a really amazing, deep bond created almost instantaneously. You go through this magical period, and now there is a wonderful connection between two people who had been strangers until only days or weeks ago.

And then the inevitable happens—typically after about four months. You move from the codependent phase into the inter-dependent phase. This is marked by the questions "Who the hell is this person, anyway???" and "What was I thinking???"

All the things that enchanted you during the first three or four months now *horrify* you.

Instead of wanting to run toward the person with open arms, you want to run like hell in the opposite direction.

We alcoholics and addicts are so in love with love and ro-mance—the sort that takes place during the first four months, the codependent phase. When the dust settles and we move into this second, questioning phase of the relationship, we just can't stand it. We feel as though we have been slapped awake after a deep dream, but the dream has now turned into a nightmare called The Other Person.

Rather than recognize that this is a natural phase of rela-tionships and that the early phase cannot continue forever, in part because it is just unbearable to what remains of their friends, addicts usually detonate the relationship right here. "I thought I found The One, but I was so wrong," they tell their friends, whom they had completely neglected during those four oceanic months. (Probably because they were finally having sex again, and lots of it.)

For those able to ride the storm of that second phase, things usually just get a little worse as we move into counter-dependence. This is where we have to prove to the other per-son *that we don't really need her.* How dumb is that? But that's what we do. This is the time when we decide we have to date other people, whether we do that or not, or sleep with other people. It's a time of testing. It's fraught. Should I stay or should I go?

If the relationship can survive *that* phase, we now move to independence. Hooray! It's the Fourth of July and fireworks are going off. Not the same kind of fireworks as in phase one, but it's still pretty exciting. The couple has weathered the storms and now can begin to think about life in an adult manner. Should we get married? What about our religious differences? What about Uncle Dexter, who does the chicken dance at every family wedding, gets drunk, and pees on the wedding cake?

And other such matters.

Here's the kicker with alcoholics and addicts: We really only like one of those four phases, and I'll bet you can guess which one it is. That's right—codependence. We *love* codependence. We love the excitement, the drama, the freshness, the passion, not to mention the torrid and constant sex. The other three phases pale by comparison. After all, we're the people who devote ourselves to getting high. So why on earth would we want to stop now? So the next time you hear someone in a meeting describe himself or herself as codependent, or label someone else as such, you'll know exactly what they're talking about. They're talking about a person who loves love. Who is only comfortable in that initial phase where all is fabulous beyond words . . . and will do anything to try to keep a relationship in that phase.

As you can imagine, those people don't make the best partners, because once the four months have come and gone, those people have come and gone, too. That's why previous generations used to have a term, *four seasons,* meaning spend *four seasons* with a person before you commit. Maybe they can ride past the codependent phase. Maybe they can't.

God help you if you are congenitally attracted to people in the oppositional or counter-dependent phase. This means that you will be forever having arguments over everything, from whether it's partly cloudy or partly sunny to which cell phone service to use. People get stuck in each of these phases. Psychologists tell us that whenever we went through early trauma, we stay stuck as adults in the same phase in which we were traumatized as children. So the smartest thing you can do is act like your grandparents and wait four seasons before you commit. Try before you buy. Try it for a year.

A *year*? I hear you saying. And besides, she's pregnant anyway!

You're right, I forgot. I'm not writing a dating manual. I'm writing a book about being a sober father. So what do you do with all this fascinating information? As Stuart Smalley used to say, take a look in the mirror. Ask yourself if everything after the first 120 days of a relationship is unsatisfying to you. If it is, you, my friend, are as codependent as the day is long. Run, don't walk, to a well-trained therapist and deal with this, because this is certainly not an issue that people in the rooms are capable of handling for you.

They're still commiserating over their broke pickers.

This is one of the things about AA that would amuse me if it weren't so dangerous—people who, only a short few months or years earlier, could not pull up their own flies, hold a job, or even floss, suddenly consider themselves, by dint of their own physical sobriety, a Dr. Phil, Dr. Drew, or even Dr. Oz when in fact they have no more psychological training than Dr. Dre.

My advice: When someone other than me is giving you advice, run like hell.

Along these lines, have you ever wondered why you could meet five thousand people over the course of a decade and yet you're only attracted enough to maybe five of them to want to marry them? Why those five?

One of the things that I found the most helpful, when I was out there dating away, was a book called *Getting the Love You Want* by Dr. Harville Hendrix.[6] His point was this: The way we were treated by our opposite sex parent—that's your mom, if I'm going too fast for you—dictates how you expect to be treated by a person with whom you are in a love relationship. If Mom was kind, you will only be interested in and attracted to kind people. If Mom was distant or verbally cruel, same thing. If you come from a home where alcoholism and substance abuse occurred, the boundaries were probably blurred.

In other words, we each might have a template built into our brains that allows us to screen for people who will treat us just the way our opposite sex parent did. So if you're in a relationship with someone and she suddenly reminds you of your mother, there's a good reason. It's because you screened out the other 4,995 people you met, and you were only attracted to her and maybe four other women, all of whom will also treat you just the way Mom did. At some points in our lives, we might relish in what we don't know. Opposites attract for a reason. However, at other times, perhaps we're drawn to that template we know all too well.

Paradoxically, we attract people who are opposite to us in some ways and yet will treat us just the way our opposite sex parent treated us. Who said reality was simple?

Hendrix's point is that until you recognize the template, you will likely continue to choose people who treat you, for better or worse, the way Mom did. You can change the template in therapy, but it's not an overnight fix. This stuff takes time. Again, this information is of no use to you now that your partner is pregnant or now that you actually have a child. You can file it away for your next life. It's worth applying to your current relationship, of course.

So is the related concept of boundaries.

One of the things you hear a lot about in Al-Anon meetings is the concept of healthy boundaries. It's a psychological term that has made its way into the heart of Al-Anon, and with good reason. Establishing healthy boundaries is one of the most important things that can happen for an individual or for a family. If you come from an alcoholic home, the boundaries were probably blurred. My point here is to shed some light on where you may have come from, so that you don't unconsciously carry unhealthy practices from your family of origin into your new life as a parent.

To put it simply, *boundaries* means knowing where I end and you begin. Remember, we've talked about the codependent phase in a baby's life, where the baby has no idea that he is a separate entity from the mother. They flow together so perfectly, and this is the dance of life that nature has created, allowing mother and newborn child to flourish.

We've seen how this pattern repeats in the early stages of a new love relationship—it's that overwhelming feeling that you've finally found the person who completes you. It's perfectly healthy, and it's delightful. But like all good things, it must end if the relationship is going to move along in a healthy fashion. As we've seen, this is where a lot of alcoholics get stuck.

We enjoy that codependent, overwhelming experience of romantic love so much that when it goes away, as it should and as it must, we feel empty. Rather than pursue the relationship in a healthy fashion into its next appropriate phase, we abandon it and look for that same sort of explosive romance with someone else.

But now you are a father, or you're about to become one. Or you have children, and now you have sobriety as well. Entering into a codependent relationship with your child is simply unfair. Your child has every right to have his or her boundaries respected. That child also deserves to live in a home with healthy boundaries present. What that means, and how to accomplish that, is the subject of this chapter.

The opposite of healthy boundaries is what psychologists call *enmeshment*. Enmeshment is a situation where two people remain stuck in that codependent phase where the boundaries are not just vague but obliterated. If I don't know where I end and you begin, we both have a problem. Typically, you see enmeshment in alcoholic homes where you've got the alcoholic father, let's say, off on his own, enjoying his primary relationship with another man (Jack Daniel's, to be specific), leaving his wife's emotional needs unmet (of course, we could reverse the genders quite easily and have the same story).

Where does the neglected wife turn for emotional fulfillment? To her children, enmeshing them into her own emotional world, using them, essentially, to fulfill her unmet needs for love and emotional connection, since her alcoholic spouse is unavailable to her in those critical ways.

In other words, the mother (or father) in this scenario isn't raising the child—she is using the child as a substitute for the emotionally unavailable parent. As you can readily imagine, this is utterly unfair to the child, who was not put on earth in order to meet his mother's unfulfilled emotional needs.

I'm not saying that we don't have a deep emotional bond with our children. I *am* saying that we do not look to them to fulfill our needs.

The reward of working the Steps in Al-Anon is detachment. *Detachment* simply means that there are healthy, appropriate boundaries in place between two people. I know where I end and you begin. I know that you are not here to satisfy my emotional needs, and you know that you do not have a responsibility to do so. As I once heard in an Al-Anon meeting, there is no Step called "detachment." Rather, detachment is what you get in Al-Anon if you take the Steps. In AA, you get sobriety. In Al-Anon,* you get detachment.

What does *detachment* mean? Ideally, it means that my emotions are not affected by your behavior. As my Al-Anon sponsor used to tell me, "The goal of the program is that other people's opinions of me don't affect my opinion of me."

The alcoholic spouse can be drinking, using, doing whatever, but if I am working a solid Al-Anon program, I am detached emotionally from that person's behavior. I am able to live my life with dignity and grace regardless of what the alcoholic is doing. It frequently happens that one member in a relationship gets so seriously and sincerely into Al-Anon that the alcoholic winds up quitting drinking.

Why? Because much of the fun of drinking, if you are an alcoholic, is having power and control over other people! If I drink and become unpredictable, I have all the power and you have none. I can scare you. I can scare the kids. I can be in control. The untreated Al-Anon, the nondrinking person in the relationship, ends up going along for the ride and, in a weird and sick way, enjoying it. Al-Anons get addicted to people the same way alcoholics get addicted to alcohol. In Al-Anon, the old-timers used to say, "Our drink has two legs."

In other words, Al-Anons, prior to recovery, get deep personal satisfaction, admittedly in a sick way, from their fascination with the drinker's behavior. They try to get them to stop drinking. They try to control them. Whatever. That's enmeshment at its worst.

---

* When I refer to Al-Anon, I can only refer to alcoholism. Strictly speaking, Al-Anon is only for those who are connected to someone with an alcohol problem.

In the home of an alcoholic or addict, pretty much every relationship reflects that same sort of enmeshment. Everybody is in each other's business. No one is allowed to live and let live. Everybody is busily trying to compulsively overcontrol everyone else, just simply as a survival tactic. Of course, everybody is miserable, and no one knows exactly why.

This is why it's so important for alcoholics (and all addicts, if there is an alcoholic somewhere in their family trees) to get into Al-Anon, but not with the typical alcoholic concept of "I can't believe I have to go to meetings with *you people*." When an alcoholic goes sincerely and with an open mind to the Al-Anon fellowship, wonderful things happen. His walls come down, and he is able to interact in a healthy manner with people, perhaps for the first time in his life.

This is why I am such a strong advocate of the Al-Anon fellowship, which certainly saved my life almost five years before I became sober.

So here we have the concepts on the table—enmeshment, which is unhealthy, and detachment and healthy boundaries, which are the goals. So what does it mean to have healthy boundaries with a child?

It means we practice the concept of "live and let live" to the best of our ability. It means that if our relationship with our spouse isn't all it could be, we don't turn to the child for emotional succor. When we do this, it's called "triangulating the child into the marriage." Children actually may enjoy this experience! That's because it's exciting, when you are a child, to be admitted to the sacred precincts of an adult relationship. Of course, it is so unhealthy for the child to be put in this position that I can't even find the words to express how wrong it is to do this. It's threatening and upsetting to the child, who somehow senses that he or she has way too much power in the home, power he or she doesn't want or need.

It's also wrong for your spouse or partner to do the same thing with your kids, but tell yourself the truth—you've pushed her into doing it because you haven't been the adult in the relationship she needs and deserves.

If your marriage isn't all that it could be, do not, repeat, do *not* turn to the child, whether your child is four, fourteen, or forty, and use him or her as an emotional crutch. This is what sponsors and therapists are for. Let your child . . . be a child. Let your child be his or her own person and not spare parts for you.

Another demonstration of enmeshment is when parents use children to send messages to the other parent, as in, "Tell your father that I'm going out tonight," or, "Tell your mother that we are out of orange juice."

It is not the child's job to be a communication service. A child is not an app.* If you have something to say to the other person, say it directly to that person. Do not involve your child as a messenger.

I remember distinctly the time that my grandmother asked me to convey a message to my father, her son. I had about six months of Al-Anon at that time, and suddenly I had a dim recognition of the fact that I had been doing this all my life for her, but it was stupid. Why couldn't she pick up the phone and call her own son? Why did she need to exert power over me in this manner?

I respectfully declined to carry the message. (That's not the message we're supposed to be carrying!) Whether she called my father and told him directly, I don't recall. I don't even remember what the situation was about. All I remember is that it

---

* That was a great line. Feel free to quote it in your five-star Amazon review of this book.

suddenly hit me that I had been used as a carrier pigeon for far too long, and it was time to stop allowing myself to be used in that manner.

In Al-Anon, we talk about different levels of detachment. There's detachment with an ax, which is often the best we can do when we are new in the fellowship. Eventually, we reach a point called detachment with love, where we are able to feel compassion for the person whose behavior seems unhealthy or inappropriate to us. It's tough to go through life when you are stuck in patterns of enmeshment and there's nothing you can do about it. That's how life was for my grandmother, who was a practicing alcoholic herself. It took a long time for me to come out of the fog of emotionally inappropriate family relationships, but eventually I did.

What about you? Was enmeshment a hallmark of your home growing up? Did one of your parents use you as a sounding board to complain about the other parent? Did your parents use you as a messenger service, as in, "Tell your father . . ." or "Tell your mother . . ."?

Were you privy to emotional truths about your parents' marriage that they shared with you, even though you were still a child?* If so, these are patterns that need to be recognized for what they are—unhealthy, and certainly not worth bringing into your relationship with your own child.

I know that we're getting a lot more deeply into our own psychology than you might have expected in this book. Maybe you thought it was just about how to order season passes for Disneyland and stuff like that. Those things are important,

---

* An adult child, in my mind, is a child who had to grow up too soon and was robbed of his or her childhood. By contrast, someone who identifies in the rooms as an "adult child" is, as I mentioned earlier, a child cleverly disguised as an adult.

and I can even tell you where to park,* but this is the real deal. When you are able to recognize that you might have been subject to the kind of enmeshment behavior I'm discussing here, it's liberating.

It doesn't make you a bad person or a weak person. It just means that you grew up in an alcoholic or drug-addicted home like the rest of us. Or maybe the home wasn't addiction prone but was unhealthy in some other way. The good news is that when you recognize patterns, you're able to stop repeating them. The last thing you want to do is take these aspects of your childhood into your role as a parent and inflict them on your child.

This is a great moment to stop and talk about language. I am not a big fan of the phrase *dysfunctional home,* which you hear bandied about in Twelve Step meeting rooms, particularly Adult Children of Alcoholics meetings and Co-Dependents Anonymous meetings. Your home may well have been dysfunctional, but let's step back for a moment and remember *that you did have a home.* Your parents may not have done the world's greatest job at providing the emotional support you needed, but let's focus on what they were able to do in terms of meeting basic needs. I'll speak for myself: My parents put three meals on the table, plus snacks, made sure I got out to school every day, clothed me, sheltered me, and took me to the dentist. In short, although I didn't realize it at the time, I was incredibly lucky in terms of what a great job they did as parents; many kids don't have that great fortune.

It's all too easy to dismiss parents as wicked and evil people, when in reality they were just adults who became parents, never got the manual, and did the best they could based on whatever

---

* Use the valet at the Grand Californian.

poor training they had received from their parents. So let's not throw around words like *dysfunctional.* Maybe it didn't function perfectly, but now that the shoe is on the other foot, let's see how perfectly your home runs! As we said from the start, perfection is the opposite of reality when it comes to being a parent. We're not even aiming for perfection; as I said earlier, we are aiming simply for "good enough."

Another term that should be banished from the vocabulary of any thinking person is the word *toxic.* Decades ago, there was a best seller called *Toxic Parents,* which made the case that such individuals were poisonous and deserving only of a harsh letter from you, the flawless human being, enumerating all of their faults. This is just plain cruel. Again, we only begin to recognize the level of sacrifice our parents made for us when we have children of our own and we are called upon to make those same sacrifices.

Poisons are toxic. People are not poisons. People are people—flawed, complicated, difficult, what have you. But please don't go around calling your parents toxic or the home in which you grew up dysfunctional. It's doing a huge disservice to people who really did their best, even though they didn't necessarily do a perfect job, or even a great job, or even a good job. They must have done something right, because here you are, so desirous of being a good father that you're actually reading a difficult book about the subject. So hats are off to you and, however grudgingly, to them.

About three fiancées ago, I took up boxing after I'd been unceremoniously dumped by the woman I thought was the love of my life. My boxing teacher would say, "If you keep dropping your hands like that, please don't tell anyone that I'm your boxing teacher."

If you're going to continue to call your family dysfunctional or your parents toxic, please don't tell anyone that you read my book. It will give them the wrong idea.

Okay, enough about the psychology of relationships.

On one of my favorite speaker tapes, the speaker says that when he was new to the program, his sponsor told him that he'd be speaking at an AA meeting.

"What do I talk about?" the newcomer asked excitedly.

"Tell them your name and then tell them you're an alcoholic," the sponsor replied, "and then sit down, because you've done told them all you know."

Well, I've done told you all I know about psychology as it applies to relationships. Recognize what *phase* you tend to get stuck in. Learn to move from *enmeshment* to *detachment,* perhaps by hanging out with those annoying Al-Anons who know so much more about relationships than you do. And stop labeling people as dysfunctional or toxic, like we're really God's gift to mental health.

And by the way, get ready, because here comes baby . . . in the very next chapter.

None of Us Feel Ready to Be a Father

The night before our first child was born, there were three of us in our apartment—my wife, her doula (or birthing assistant), and me.* By 7:00 that night, my wife had been in labor for more than twenty-four hours. Early labor consists of mild contractions every five to ten minutes, with intervals between contractions gradually decreasing. We did everything her birthing class had taught her: We went for a walk at a meditation retreat. I gave her a massage. We hung out. But after twenty-seven hours, I was starting to go a little bit bonkers. Like most alcoholics, I don't do patience very well.

I called up one of my mentor figures in the program. He told me to come out and he would buy me dinner. So I told my wife that I was going out to grab a bite and I would be back in an hour.

When I tell this story now, men nod and say that makes sense. You needed a break.

Women look at me as if I'm the devil. How could I have abandoned my wife?

So I don't tell women this story anymore.

(In my own defense: *I did not abandon her.* Instead, I left her in the company of her doula, a woman who would prove far

---

* Four, if you count the baby.

more useful and involved over the next twelve hours than I, the loving husband.)

My AA friend John and I met in a Santa Monica delicatessen. Over a tuna sandwich, I confessed, "John, I don't think I'm ready to be a father."

I was forty-one years old.

I don't think any man is thoroughly ready to be a father until the baby actually arrives. It's not until you actually see that little person that the whole thing moves from the realm of theory. But even before the baby makes her arrival, there's still plenty to be done. There are three subject matter areas where husbands must be supremely useful in the months that lead to the birth of the child. We could shorthand them with these words: **near, gear,** and **fear.**

Be **near**by. You know how you've always wanted to hike the Appalachian Trail or climb a mountain in South America? What a perfect time, right? Your wife's pregnant, she may not be that into sex, and she's got all her girlfriends to take care of her, right?

Wrong. This is not the time to go to Machu Picchu. This is the time to begin to accept the responsibility that she will be looking to you at all times and for all purposes.

She may *say* that it doesn't matter all that much if you choose not to accompany her to her Lamaze breathing classes or meet with her baby doctor.

She is lying.

She wants you to show up for everything, and more than that, she wants you to show up willingly, happily, and with the intent of engaging seriously. You showed up for the unprotected sex. She expects you now to show up for everything else.

There are four reasons why you want to show up for all the sessions. First, the last thing your partner wants to feel, as she goes through pregnancy, is alone and unsupported. Your presence is everything. You might think that she would be happier going with a girlfriend who will understand better, perhaps one who has already given birth. But that's not how it works. She wants *you*. I can't speak from the inside, but my guess is that a woman's fears of abandonment reach their zenith during pregnancy.

She doesn't feel as sexy. She might fear that the responsibility will be too much for you and you'll bolt. Showing up for everything pregnancy- and childbirth-related is a great way of silently assuaging those fears.

The next reason why you want to be there is that you actually play a role. Your partner might want you to serve as her breathing coach. That means that you're going to guide her and keep her breathing on track as she approaches the moment of delivery. It's a big responsibility, and you cannot just read the manual on the way to the hospital (especially if you're driving, and few women about to give birth really want to take the wheel). There are also important decisions to be made about the nature of the birth plan. *How* will she deliver? In a hospital? In a birthing center? At home? In water? Don't laugh—all of these are options today.

It's ultimately your partner's call, but she may want your opinion, or more likely, your support. Going to the hospital and doing things the traditional way is no longer the requirement. Get educated along with your partner. You might just have some useful input, but even if you don't, your presence is everything.

A third reason for rearranging your calendar so that you can attend breathing classes and doctors' appointments is that not everything goes right.

I accompanied my wife for every single one of her ultrasounds on all of her successful pregnancies, and I'm glad I did. We were fortunate in that all of our children came out fine, but you just never know. Every time we went in for an ultrasound, the nurse would say, "I have good news. Your baby doesn't have . . ." and then she would name three or four or five truly horrific-sounding diseases or conditions. When people think about having a baby, they think about having a *healthy* baby. The reality isn't always what one pictures. So if there is bad news—if an ultrasound or an amnio or some other test reveals something amiss—*you have to be there with her to hear the news.* You may or may not feel bad about yourself if you miss a healthy checkup, but you will feel like a jerk, and rightly so, if you miss one where the news is not good.

I'm not trying to alarm you. Most of the time, things go fine. But not every time. So don't take a chance and skip something.

The fourth and final reason for showing up is all about *you.* (Finally.)

This is your child, too, after all. This is your opportunity to share in moments that are truly unforgettable. If you've never been to an ultrasound, this is the opportunity for you and your partner to peek in on your unborn child, as he or she quietly gestates away inside the womb. Imaging technology—especially 3-D technology—lets you see so much—the head, the spine, limbs, even fingers and toes toward the end of the pregnancy. This is the first time that the baby's heartbeat can be detected. Where else would you rather be? In your cubicle at work? At the gym?

I will never forget the awesome moment on February 1, 2002—my tenth AA birthday, as it happens—at about 10:30 in the morning when my wife and I went to her OB/GYN's office, expecting to learn the gender of our second child. The nurse applied the gel to my wife's abdomen, put the ultrasound device next to her skin, and we waited nervously for the news. And then she said those life-changing words: "I see two."

Two babies.

Twins.

The room began to spin.

We were on the sixth floor of a hospital building.

"Does that window open?" I asked hoarsely.

"Do you need some air?" the nurse asked.

"No," I replied. "I want to jump."

I didn't, and now the two little agglomerations of consciousness are fourteen-year-old boys who go to school, play ball, make YouTube videos, and sometimes make us crazy. Would I have wanted to miss that moment of discovery?

Would you?

As a side note, since my wife was over the age of thirty, the protocol was to follow up with 3-D imaging, which was the actual point when we discovered the gender of the twins. Both boys. That was on a Thursday.

Two days later, I was at synagogue when I recognized the doctor who had performed the 3-D ultrasound on my wife. I was carrying the "baby pictures" of my sons in my pocket, and I took them out and showed them to him.

"I just did this guy's wife!" the doctor shouted happily, waving the photos for all to see, and earning a confused look from the rabbi.

Be there. That's the bottom line.

This applies to all situations involving bringing a new young person into your home, by whatever means apply. She's got an appointment at an infertility clinic?

That means you both have an appointment at the clinic. Together.

Be there.

With the adoption agency?

Be there.

Be there, be there, be there.

Then, get the **gear.**

It's amazing how someone who isn't even born yet can cause so much dislocation . . . and shopping.

Babies are gear-intensive. You'll need a car seat if you expect to get the little darling home from the hospital legally (and safely). You'll need a crib, a changing table, diapers (cloth or disposable), wipes, a heater to heat the wipes (get it, trust me), and on and on until your mind is empty and your credit card is full. Just deal with it.

If you're wondering how you're going to pay for all that, and you see yourself stealing cartons of Pampers from the 7-Eleven, take heart. There's an expression in the Jewish tradition I want to share with you—"Babies create their own *mazal*," or good luck. If you've got the guts to have a child, God will make sure you have the money to support it.

Especially if you have a job.

If your partner is anything like my wife, she's going to spend an enormous amount of time reading through reviews of all the aforementioned gear. Help her if she wants help, and if she doesn't, then go to the mall with her and buy the stuff, and help her carry it home. Again, this is a wonderful way to express wordlessly your commitment to her and to the family you are building. You're not going to get a medal for doing any of these things. You will enjoy, however, the intense satisfaction of knowing that you are showing up and doing the right thing.

Finally, **fear.** I've never been pregnant, but my wife and I have been through five pregnancies, three that worked out and two that didn't. My wife is pretty levelheaded (unlike myself). Pregnancy is scary. The body goes through change after change.

There are no guarantees that everything is going to work out. And knowing that you've got to deliver a child, whether you've done it before or not, is a fearsome fact.

Now *you* try that on for size.

Those are her fears. You've most likely got yours as well. For me, they included the following: What kind of father will I be? Will I be like my own (still drinking) dad? Will the baby be okay? Will I be able to make the money to pay for this? What if . . . what if . . . what if . . . , and you can fill in the "what if" with anything.

It was my job as a sober member of Alcoholics Anonymous to process my fears with someone other than my wife. This meant writing an inventory, reading it to my sponsor, acknowledging my part, identifying the character defects (or bad habits) involved, and saying the Seventh Step prayer to give them to my Higher Power. I did that over and over. If I hadn't done that, then on any given day, there's an excellent chance that my unprocessed fears would have infected the way I related to my wife. I would have been agitated or upset, and more likely to snap at her. I couldn't have been the best possible me.

I also took to asking my Higher Power to walk in the door with me when I went home after work, because I knew that the whole thing was too much for me to manage on my own. But why should I even try? That's the whole point of the program, isn't it? To know that you're not alone, that you don't have to figure things out by yourself, and that there is a loving, caring Higher Power who will get you through anything? As my longtime sober friend Sean M. says, "God has your picture on His refrigerator."*

---

* Sean, if you're reading this, you owe me a phone call.

So rather than get my wife upset, or trigger whatever fear and anxiety she might have had, my responsibility as a sober father-to-be was to take care of my own emotions in a healthy setting, with my sponsor or with another AA friend. That way, I could show up as my best possible self, and that, after all, was and remains my job.

My favorite college professor fell in love with a man who had two teenage children from a prior marriage living with him.

When she moved in with them, I asked her what it was like to suddenly have to relate to the two young teens.

Her answer: "I think of them as my young friends."

That conversation, more than thirty-five years ago, dictates how I view my children.

Yes, I'm their parent and not their schoolmate or friend from camp.

And yes, I'm responsible for setting limits and discipline and all that stuff.

At the same time, however, I enjoy a friendship with each of them.

A friendship of course that reflects the role I play as their father.

And yet, on a good day, when it's not about setting limits or saying no ice cream before bed or any of that Daddy-like behavior, there is a friendship growing that I hope will continue long after they are out of the house.

Moving on.

Our daughters were born via natural childbirth, but due to the positions of our sons in the womb, they had to be delivered via cesarean. I put on a cap and gown and sat alongside my wife, who was thoroughly sedated but wide awake and extremely comfortable. On the other side of what looked like a Ping-Pong net, the doctor was operating away. If you've never witnessed a cesarean section, think back to the *Itchy & Scratchy* cartoons on *The Simpsons*.

The births went fine—the boys were born, or, more accurately, removed, from inside my wife, in a perfectly normal manner. They had me cut the two umbilical cords. It was wild. So now I'm sitting beside her once again and it just seems as though the doctor is getting more and more flustered as he's sewing her up.

My wife doesn't notice this, but I certainly do. She's just chatting away, oblivious to the drama surrounding her. I write a note to the anesthesiologist. "Is everything okay?" I pass him the note. He reads it and scribbles a response.

"No."

There was some complication, most likely, a doctor friend later explained, a hemorrhage of some sort due to the pressure of the fetuses on, um, something in my wife's body.

Clearly medical school is not part of my story.

All of a sudden the room starts to spin. I give my wife a charming smile and tell her that I need to step outside and get a little air.

What is going on? I have no idea. I just know that if I stay in there, with the room spinning faster and faster, I'll need anesthesiology, too.

They take me outside the room and I explain what's going on with me. They have me sit on the floor and they give me a cup of water. So there I am in my hospital cap and gown when a tour of the new hospital residents comes through. It's mid-July, and they've just arrived to take up their responsibilities.

"That's what it looks like," the group leader says, pointing to me sitting on the floor with my cup of water, "when you become a father of twins."

My wife came out just fine, by the way. Thank you, God.

But back to you.

None of us *feel* ready. That's because there's a "baby code" we don't know yet. Are you ready to crack the baby code?

Babies don't speak English. In fact, they don't speak at all. When they're upset, they cry.

It doesn't mean that they are existentially upset that you are their father. Don't take it personally.

When babies cry, it probably means that they are wet, hungry, or tired.

(Just like Dad.)

Change the baby's diaper.

Feed the baby.

Hold the baby.

Put her on your chest.

Tell her how much you love her.

Tell your partner how much you love the baby.

Tell your partner how much you love her (your partner), too.

Remember that everyone will be oohing and aahing over the baby.

While neglecting your wife.

So give her things and experiences—a beautiful nightgown to remind her that you still think she's sexy.

Massages.

A day of beauty at the spa.

Whatever she wants.

And that's how you crack the baby code—just show up, try to figure out what they need even if they can't verbalize those needs (that goes for the baby and for your partner), get some sleep while you can, and hang in there.

Is it really that simple?

For sober dads, yes. If we do the things in this chapter, we'll be fine.

(Good news: and so will the baby!)

Your Kids Will Ask about God, So It's Time to Figure Out Your Answers

Okay, so now your kids are talking (and probably talking back).

You'll have all kinds of intriguing conversations with them as they ask you questions that are anywhere from enchanting to unanswerable.

Like, "Why do I have to have a baby brother?"

And, "How many trees are there in the world?"

Memo to dads: It's okay to say, "That's a good question. I don't know."

By the time you've found an answer on Wikipedia, however, your child will have forgotten the question and really just want some chocolate milk.

Unless the question was *The Question*—who or what exactly is this God thing, anyway?

This might just be the most delicate subject in the book, because not only are we talking about my conception of a Higher Power, but we're also talking about yours, and then the unique conception of a Higher Power that belongs, or will belong, to each of your children.

So before we can figure out how to answer that question, let's first step back and see what God means to us.

Alcoholics Anonymous defines alcoholism as a threefold disease—a physical compulsion combined with a mental obsession, leading to a spiritual loss of values. As we have discussed, AA is not a program with a spiritual angle; it is a spiritual program. It has been said that the purpose of Alcoholics Anonymous is simply to bring the alcoholic back to God.

In other words, there came a point in our lives where we needed to become sober, and at that point, or soon thereafter, we realized we needed God.

As the Twelve and Twelve says, we realized we had to stop playing God to our fellows.

We had to stop living as if there were no God and, as is written in the Bible, "men could do whatever was right in their own eyes."

We needed to find a spiritual path.

Carl Jung, the psychologist who so deeply influenced Bill Wilson, one of the cofounders of AA, called alcohol "a low-level quest for God"—which is why another word for alcohol is *spirits*.

Of all the things that sober parents desire in life, probably the greatest desire, tied to the greatest fear, is that their children do not develop addiction problems of their own.

I'm not qualified to weigh in on the question of genetics. From what I've read, genetics play an important role in determining whether one will end up an addict. But I don't think that genetics are the equivalent of a death sentence, that someone with an alcoholic parent is also destined to become an alcoholic or addict.

I would like to believe that this is not the case and that the parents have an opportunity to affect the future of their children with regard to alcoholism and addiction the same way they affect so much else of a child's future.

So if the solution in Alcoholics Anonymous comes down to finding a Higher Power and accepting and acting on spiritual help, doesn't it stand to reason that the most important gift we could give our own children is the gift of spirituality? Don't we have a responsibility, in other words, to bring a Higher Power into the home and to model what it means to live a spiritual life?

One of the things that appealed to me about Alcoholics Anonymous is what you could call "everyday spirituality."

The beauty of the Judeo-Christian ethos, which Alcoholics Anonymous echoes, is that you can be spiritual anywhere, anytime. You don't need to go off to a mountaintop where there are no other people. You don't need to abandon your family and the life you know. Instead, you can be spiritual in your own home, in the way you drive, in the way you operate in the workplace as a "worker among workers." In short, in every facet of your life.

I'm reminded of a song lyric I love (and used to live by): "One day of praying and six nights of fun. The odds against going to heaven: six-to-one."

That's not how we live now that we're clean and sober! Instead, we alcoholics and addicts accept upon ourselves the yoke of heaven, and we devote ourselves to seeking God's will and developing the power to carry it out, as we say in our Eleventh Step. So the question then becomes, how do you bring God into the conversation with your children, in such a way that you are enhancing their spirituality as opposed to forcing it down their throats?

A buddy of mine, the same one who insisted on showing me the video of his wife giving birth, had the best line of all about this. "We haven't decided," he told me, "how much religion we're going to inflict on our child."

My in-laws, who are Buddhist, once sent their son, then five years old, to a Christian summer camp.

At the family dinner the following week, the father said to the son, "Do you want to thank Jesus for your food?"

The boy was furious. "I don't want to thank Jesus!" he shouted. "You can't make me thank Jesus! I'm not gonna thank Jesus!"

And he *didn't* thank Jesus.

So it's all about walking that fine line where we're not inflicting religious beliefs on our children, and yet at the same time we are seeking to guide them on a spiritual path.

One of my all-time favorite books is called *Type A Behavior and Your Heart* by Meyer Friedman and Ray H. Rosenman,[7] two San Francisco cardiologists who invented the term *Type A* to describe the constellation of character traits that make up the heart-attack-prone individual.

They wrote, "Never in human history have so many people sought to live in so deep a spiritual void."

They didn't write those words last year. They wrote them in the early 1960s.

If they think that was a spiritual void, what do they think of the world today? And this is the world in which we are raising our children.

Before we talk about how to introduce the subject of a Higher Power, it's important that we do a quick gut check on where you are with yours.

Some people come to Twelve Step recovery with a happy concept of a Higher Power. I'm working with a newcomer right now who is a regular churchgoer and feels very comfortable with God. For him, the new thing is asking God to help him with his alcoholism. That's something he's never done before, but it's fine with him.

I wasn't like that. I came into my first Twelve Step program, Al-Anon, with a decidedly negative view of God. To me, God was like a highway patrolman sitting on his motorcycle, hiding behind a billboard, ready to catch you for speeding or some other violation. He didn't exactly have your best interests at heart.

(No offense meant to motorcycle cops, by the way.)

Why did I have such a negative view of God? I could share with you some of my family history. All of my mother's relatives, except for her immediate family, uncle, and aunt, were murdered in the Holocaust. We have family albums full of pictures of children who never saw adulthood because they were killed in the camps.

My mother's father, who was prescient enough to get his family out of Europe when the war began, was murdered in a holdup—it was actually a mob hit—when he was sixty and I was ten. My family collapsed around my brokenhearted grandmother, and her well-being was the focal point of my mother's life for the next four-and-a-half years, until she died of breast cancer, but more accurately, a broken heart.*

And now you in Twelve Step Land are telling me that there's a loving God whom I should trust?

Not buying it.

As a result, I had developed two highly negative attitudes toward God. One was anger for all the things that had gone on in our family, in the families of other people, and in the world, and the other was shame. I did a lot of things that I'm not proud of while I was drinking. I'm not about to start listing them, but you can probably guess what those sorts of things might be. So

---

* This was also my victimhood story—combine that with my father's alcoholism and emotional abandonment of the family, and of course I drank. This gave me license to do anything I wanted and to use people however I saw fit. Who was there for me? So why should I be there for you?

if God were watching through some celestial peephole, I was screwed.

So how exactly was I to do business, as we say in the rooms, with a Higher Power, given what had gone on and given what I had done?

I mention all this not out of some exhibitionistic streak (although the definition of an extrovert is that nothing really happens to him until he tells someone else about it).

I mention all this because there's a possibility that you may have not yet fully come to terms with the concept of a Higher Power. So I thought that maybe the solutions I found might help you, so that when your children start asking you questions, you are in your comfort zone when you give answers.

In many Twelve Step meeting groups, there's no culture of getting the newcomer into the Steps, our insurance policy against drinking and using. The Steps are the means by which we develop spiritually, so that we never have to drink again, a day at a time, and so that we can become the people our Higher Power intended us to be.

And yet, we seem to have entered a post-Steps version of AA when you go to many meetings. People get a round of applause when they mention their day count. Why does no one get a round of applause when he announces that he's taken the Third Step? Because we never ask who's taken the Third Step, or any Step.

This gives the newcomer an inaccurate representation of recovery. Not emphasizing the Steps suggests to the newcomer that all you have to do is go to enough meetings, and knit together enough days, and eventually you will be stone-cold sober, with all the rights and privileges pertinent thereto.

That's just not how it works. Time is terrific—as my sponsor says, who would you rather have flying a plane, a pilot with twenty-five years' experience or one who's been flying for only twenty-five days? So time matters. But real recovery is a function of taking the Steps and helping others through the Steps. Time doesn't accrue by itself.

That's why we're hitting the pause button on our parenting discussion and taking a moment to affirm where you are with your Higher Power. Without that security blanket (serenity blanket?) in place, your sobriety is tenuous. And now, like the Michelin Man, there's a lot riding on you.

So here's what happened with me when I got to the Third Step for the first time and had to confront that decision about whether to let a Higher Power into my life. As I quoted Chuck C. earlier, God is a gentleman—he doesn't go where he isn't invited.

My Al-Anon sponsor, Harv, asked me to describe my Higher Power.

I thought for a moment and told him about the motorcycle cop behind the billboard. Then I told him that God was maybe present at one point but was no longer especially present now. He was distant, not listening, not especially caring about me or about the world.

Harv listened thoughtfully. Then he said something that absolutely blew me away.

"Now tell me what your father was like when he was drinking."

Suddenly I realized that my concept of God was identical to my experience of my father when he was drunk. All the things that I mentioned about God summed up my father, in his cups, to a T.

Harv, who now had me where he wanted me, asked a follow-up question.

"If you could invent God, and you cannot, what would God be like?"

I thought for another moment.

"Loving," I began. "Caring. Present. Listening to me. There for me."

Harv grinned.

"Shake hands with your new Higher Power," he said.

Bottom line: I had to have a healthy relationship with a Higher Power before I could become a healthy Higher Power to my own children.

The cliché in the rooms is that all you have to know about God is that you aren't it, and that's a good starting point. But it really does help to have some sort of concept that works for you. It doesn't have to be my concept of God. It doesn't have to be your sponsor's. And it doesn't even have to be your child's. In some ways, a definition of God is an oxymoron. How can you define the undefinable? That's why something inside me always laughs quietly when we read the words "as we understood him" in the Steps.

We don't understand him. As it says in the Psalms, quoting God (how'd they do that?), "My thoughts are not like your thoughts."

I would never have had the courage to create a world where people had free will. We'd end up with what we have today. So clearly I don't understand God, and I don't have the slightest idea about why the world is the way it is. All I know, to paraphrase Chevy Chase, is that God's God, and I'm not.

I also know that the world has the capacity to be a beautiful, loving place, if only people could stop messing things up. And that led to the first breakthrough I had after that conversation with Harv, which put me on the path toward a relationship with God.

I realized that 95 percent of the things that had happened to me, to my relatives, to others, were situations where people misused their free will. I misused my free will and hurt people. I never killed anyone, but I certainly hurt people, and sometimes, on an emotional level, severely. So now I realized that if I was to be intellectually honest, I could not blame God for the things I had done to other people, and therefore, *I could not blame God for the things other people had done to my family or to me.*

I mentioned that 95 percent of the things that have happened were people misusing their free will. The other 5 percent is tragedy. I don't fully understand the purpose of tragedy, although I certainly understand that it is a powerful teacher. In my understanding of things, the existence of tragedy does not disprove the existence of God. In other words, maybe God allows tragedy to happen for reasons that we cannot necessarily understand at the moment.

The other half of my problem with God came down to the shame I felt for the things I had done that hurt other people. There's an Eighth and a Ninth Step in every Twelve Step program that requires us to make amends to the people we hurt. I did that. I did that to the best of my ability, and I would like to think that in most cases my amends were accepted. I also practice what we call a living amends, which means that when I am in the same situations where I hurt people in the past, I don't behave the same way.

This is how I was able to reduce and eventually all but eliminate the anger and shame I felt with regard to my Higher Power. As a result, I was finally able, as we like to say, to do business with God.

As a result, when my kids were very small and began to ask the kid questions—which are actually brilliant questions—like where did the world come from, and why is there air, and where did you and Mommy come from, and where do babies come from, I was able to say, without feeling like a hypocrite or a presidential candidate,* "They come from God."

It is amazing how accepting small children are of the idea that there is a creator. They intuitively understand that everything comes from something, so why not the universe? It's my experience that people who do have faith find life easier to bear than those who don't. Speaking of presidential candidates, I write these words during a highly combustible presidential campaign season. One of my closest friends, a devout Christian, is the first cousin of a candidate who was expected to win his party's nomination and instead flamed out ignominiously. I asked my friend how his cousin was doing.

"He's fine," came the surprising response.

"How could he be fine? Think about all the money he went through."

"He believes that God has a plan," my friend said. "He's playing a lot of golf with his son these days."

To me, that sounds like a lot more fun than running for president.

As my kids have gotten older, their questions have become more sophisticated. My favorite was when my daughter asked how God became God. She decided that there must have been a ghost raffle.

I'll wait while you think that one through.

I attend religious services regularly. My kids have seen me do this since time out of mind. With each of them, I thought back to what my first AA sponsor said about caterpillars and butterflies. He said that when a caterpillar enters a chrysalis

---

* Same thing, of course.

in order to transform itself into a butterfly, the natural human reaction might be to reach in to try to "help."

Helping, under those circumstances, means killing the creature. No butterfly. No nothing.

I've taken the same approach with the development of my children's spirituality. I've just figured that they are each in their own spiritual chrysalis, and that if I reach in and try to force God on them, or as my friend with the video camera said, inflict too much religion on them, I will kill their chances of having a healthy spiritual life before it has time to take root.

Occasionally, I'll just start, out of the blue, maybe in the car, where I have a captive audience, talking about how grateful I am to God for giving us health and life and resources, enough that we actually can do some of the extras that parents want to provide for their children. What they do with those brief outbursts I have no idea. I'm hoping that they file them away, so that they can develop their own healthy approach to spirituality as they grow.

Start early. The sooner you get your kids (and yourself) in a routine involving regular attendance at religious services, the easier it will be for you (and them). Yes, it's boring for kids, but this is the way pretty much every religion or spiritual practice makes room for the next generation. Allow your kids to develop their own spiritual lives when young. Don't make them wait until they get sober, if that's their path. A spiritual life will allow them to get through tough situations that arise in childhood. It will also allow them to realize that there's something bigger in the world than them and their needs. Most religious institutions encourage the practice of charitable giving, and the sooner your kids make that a part of their lives, the better off they—and the world—will be.

Look, they will believe what they believe. They will affiliate religiously however they see fit. My job as their father in this circumstance is to open the door for them, make spiritual and religious training available to them—at this writing, three of our four children attend religious schools, and the one who doesn't want to, doesn't—and let them make up their own minds.

My sponsor once asked me, "Who knows more about God than you do?"

At first I thought he was referring to the fact that I had spent a year or so in a Jerusalem seminary. Then I had that forehead-slapping moment when I realized that no human being knows anything more about God than any other.

When I was new, there was a speaker on a cassette tape that I played over and over and over. One of the things he said that affected me the most—I believe the speaker was Tom from Santa Monica: "No one is any closer to God today than the day he or she entered Alcoholics Anonymous, and no one in this room is closer to God than anyone else in the room. The only difference is the awareness of the nearness that was there all the time."

It's been my experience in recovery that what the Big Book says is true—that God does not make too hard a bargain with those who want to communicate with him, and the more of a relationship I want to have with God, the more available God suddenly becomes.

In short, as a sober dad, it's up to me to model for my children a healthy relationship with a Higher Power. After that, all I can do, and all that I suggest that you do, is to open the door for them and then step out of their way.

Embrace Being a
Perfectly Imperfect Dad

Time to let go of perfectionism.

The good news is that you don't have to be perfect to be a wonderful father.

You just have to be, in Bruno Bettelheim's formulation, good enough.

Think for a moment about how freeing it would be not to have to be perfect as a parent.

Instead of aiming for being *perfect,* aim for being *loving.*

In this chapter, let's talk about strategies for letting go of perfectionism on the one hand and demonstrating your loving-kindness on the other.

My sponsor had four kids. He said with the first one, he would sterilize the bottle, weigh the milk, and so on, being totally perfectionistic about everything.

By the fourth kid, he was rolling a dirty bottle across the floor to the kid. I'm not sure that's the recommended path, either, but you get my point. I'm not suggesting you slack off. I am saying that there's a middle ground between perfectionism and lack of interest, and it's up to you to find that sweet spot.

You also don't have to be a perfect husband.

One of the themes of this book has been that an attentive husband makes for a happier wife and a happier home. But let's get real. Having a baby is stressful. You're not sleeping. You're not in your normal routines. Your parents are butting in constantly with their own useless opinions. Friends are dropping by unexpectedly, as if the baby were a new Picasso you acquired. You're not having nearly as much sex as before, or if you are, it's mostly with yourself. So I understand you're a little bit on edge.

Interestingly, the Tenth Step of Alcoholics Anonymous—not to go Step Warrior on you—says, and I quote, "And when we were wrong." Not "and if we were wrong."

"And *when* we were wrong."

We're going to be wrong. We're going to say the wrong thing. We're going to do the wrong thing. We're going to screw up. Over and over. There's a learning curve to being a parent. But it's okay. You don't have to be perfect. Just give it your best shot, and when you say the wrong thing, or do the wrong thing, apologize as quickly as you can.

Do you ever apologize to your child? I have, from the time that I had to get on my knees to be able to look them in the eye. There's nothing wrong with apologizing to a child. You don't want to stand on ceremony with your own kid and pretend you're perfect.

I have a standard of telling each one of them, every single day, that I love them. Now, do they need to hear that over and over again?

It's like chicken soup. It couldn't hurt.

Zig Ziglar, the late, great motivational speaker and author, said that he met the head of the Department of Corrections of a southern state, who told him that he had eighty thousand inmates in his system and only eleven Jews.[8] Ziglar reported this to an audience, and at the end of the speech, a man came up to him and told him that he was the head of the Department of Corrections for another state. He told Zig that out of forty thousand inmates, they only had thirteen Jews. Not to be out-done, the head of Corrections for a third state came over to Ziglar and told him that in his system there were thirty-five thousand inmates and only nine Jews.

So Ziglar did some research to find out what went on in Jewish homes that could be an explanation for the exceedingly low incarceration rates among Jewish people.*

He said that Jewish fathers do three things on a constant basis.

First, they tell their sons that they love them on a regular basis.

Next, they bless their sons every Friday night at the Sabbath table.

Third, after they finish giving their sons a blessing at the Sabbath table—for the record, we bless our daughters, too—Jewish fathers kiss their children, hug them, and tell them, "I love you."

If you are told on a regular basis that you are loved, you are less likely than average to end up in a correctional institution.

So take all that energy that you are saving, now that you no longer have to be a perfectionistic parent, and use it to hug your children, kiss them, and, yes, bless them. You don't have to be Jewish to bless your kids. Just tell them that you love them and that their Higher Power loves them.

Giving your child a spiritual foundation in today's crazy world is at least as important as making sure they get a good education or that they floss. Doesn't that seem like a good use of all that mental energy that you'll save by not having to be a perfectionist?

---

* My cynical mind suggested that we Jews simply have better lawyers.

Earlier in this book, we asked, what does a good son do? We found that the list is pretty short—you don't have to do that many things to be a good son. Call once in a while. Send a note or a card. Remember birthdays. Send flowers or a gift. Visit. And so on.

(Jewish joke time: A guy calls his Jewish mother and says, "How are you, Ma?"

"I haven't eaten in forty-six days," comes the response.

"Ma, how come?" the son asks in anguish.

"So I wouldn't have food in my mouth when you call!"

As Larry the Cable Guy says, I don't care who you are. That's funny.)

So what does a good father do?

He plays less golf.

What do I mean by that?

There's a great expression—a man can be great at golf, at being a family man, and at making a living, but he can only pick two of the three.

In short, this is the time for you to focus. Don't get off on a tangent about "they need me to make more money." They need you to show up. I understand they cannot live on love and that money makes the world go round and that it doesn't grow on trees and all those other stupid things that people say.

But here's the thing. If you throw yourself into your work now, all you're doing is distancing yourself from your feelings and from the responsibilities you need to face at this time. So make a living, but don't make making a living your life.

What else does a good father do? He is present. He is attentive to his wife. He spends large quantities of time with his child or children, because the concept of "quality time"—the idea that you could helicopter in, spend a short amount of time with your kid and make a big impression, and then scoot out again—

is nonsense. Your kid doesn't need quality time or a new hoverboard. Hey, he's only six weeks old! What he needs is you.

And don't say, "He's too young to know or care who I am."

How could we possibly have any idea what goes through the mind of a small child? Your child is learning to trust you and your partner. He is getting a sense of what psychologists call object constancy—if he makes a noise, the same people come. My heart breaks when I hear about day care centers where young children get attached to their caregivers, who suddenly vanish, and suddenly there's a new one, and then three months later, yet another one replaces the second one.

Children need consistency from caregivers. The good thing is that you learned how to be consistent by working a program. A day at a time, you do the necessary things to maintain your sobriety. Now, you're just doing a different set of things every day, in order to create a sense of consistency in the mind of your small child.

Do hug and kiss your child, boy or girl, young or old. And don't tell me, "That's not how I was raised." I don't care how you were raised.

How'd the way you were raised work out for you? It worked out so great that you became an addict.

All I know is that people like to be held and touched. Take everything you don't like about your childhood, throw it out the window, and start over. You cannot kiss your child often enough. You cannot hug her often enough. You cannot tell your child "I love you" often enough.

This goes for your wife, too, by the way—you ought to be doing the same things with her. Wives sometimes feel neglected because the husbands (and everyone else) are all about the baby. We men don't like to feel neglected. Neither do our partners. So show up for them, too. It's just common sense.

So what are the other things that children need, whether they are babies or high school students?

What are the other simple things that you need to do on a daily basis? How about reading to your child every day? This is one of the most important things you can do for a kid. Reading is a lifelong habit, but mostly for people who are read to as children. Don't you think your children will have a broader knowledge base, be more interested in the world, do better in school, and just have a more interesting, meaningful life if you read to them every day and they get into that habit themselves down the road?

Count on it.

Note to self: Read to your child every day.

I sometimes see moms at the library bringing home twelve to fifteen books at a time. It seems as though their interest is in cramming their children's brains with as many stories as they possibly can, which is just simply preparation for all those dreadful after-school enrichment classes those poor kids will have to take later on.

There's nothing wrong with a child having a favorite book, whether that child is two years old and it's something to do with frogs or bears, or the child is twelve years old and it's *Diary of a Wimpy Kid*. I'm not a big fan of reading the kid six thousand books a year—you're not loading software. It's not about following a tiger mom or tiger dad agenda to make them scary smart. It's just a nice way to bond. I'm home most weeknights, because I choose to be home most weeknights. And I am reading and/or lying down with my kids every night I'm home. It's a really nice feeling when I'm lying down on the big bed and all four of the kids are sprawled out in different positions. We're all talking. Maybe I'm reading something. Maybe I'm reading a book and changing all the words so that the story gets a tiny bit naughty. I love making them laugh.

The main thing is that you want to create as many beautiful moments for your children as you can. It doesn't take much more than a book and an arm around your child to give him or her a sense of being valued.

I tell my children I treasure them. I tell them that because it's true, and I want them to know it. Even though they've heard it a thousand times before. It's said that by the time a child is twelve or thirteen, the age of counter-dependence and adolescent rebellion, the hay is in the barn. Meaning that all the parenting you ever hoped to do with them—it's done. If you haven't gotten your message across to them, you're not going to be able to start now.

That's why from the time that they are tiny, you want to reiterate to them exactly the message that you want them to take from their childhood as a whole—that they are loved. That they are worthy of being loved. That they are wonderful. That they are a gift from God. That they are just what you wanted.

I had a client who, from a standing start, became a billionaire. His father adored him and would say, "Everybody loves Larry." My client became a billionaire because everybody trusted him and loved him. Why did they love him? Not only was he lovable, but he knew that he was *worthy* of love. He heard it from his father, so it must have been true!

Anything our parents tell us is true, because they are so powerful that, well, if it weren't true, why would they have said it? My sober buddy Jerry D., with whom I did jail panels for years, always asks the inmates, "How many of you had parents who told you you'd end up in jail one day?"

Pretty much all the hands go up.

Sigh.

If you'll remember, earlier in the book, I quoted Harville Hendrix to the effect that a person is attracted to people who will treat them the same way their opposite sex parent did. Not only does this mean that the woman you chose to marry met the template that your mother had unconsciously created for you, unless you got some good therapy and changed your template, but what you do as a father dictates who your daughter is going to marry one day.

I took Hendrix's advice to mean that as a father, with every word and gesture, with every tone of voice and with every look of my eyes, I was training my daughter on how she should be treated by men when she came of age. Maybe my daughter will sometimes look for the very opposite of me, but if she will also unconsciously look for someone who treats her like I do, then my every action carries weight. So fathers, recognize that with your daughters, *you are constantly preparing them for the next man.* But it's just as important that you treat your sons well, too.

Next. Keep in mind the wonderful expression I first heard on an Earl Nightingale audio once upon a time:[9] "What you're doing speaks so loudly that I can hardly hear a word you are saying."

In other words, don't come around here with the idea that you can tell your kids one thing and you can do something else yourself. They will see the difference, and they will despise you for it. And then they will despise themselves as well. If there is a disparity between your words and your actions, your actions will always matter more to them. You cannot tell them that they must be loving and respectful if you are not loving and respectful toward their mother, whether you are married to her or whether you never saw her again after that one fabulous night. The children are always watching, always listening, and always recording. They may not be able to put into words exactly what they are taking from you. They may be too young even to have words to use. But they are always watching and always recording.

And if that re-triggers your perfectionist tendencies, you're not alone. It's natural to feel that you want to get it absolutely right, so that you don't screw up your kids. The simple reality is that we all mess up our kids to some degree, but it's survivable. When I came out of my childhood, I hit the ground and stayed down for seventeen years, until I got sober. My goal with my children is that when they come of age, they can hit the ground running.

They will be able to do so not because I was perfect, but because I was always trying to do the best I could. When I was wrong, I promptly admitted it. Still do. By not having to be perfect, by modeling humble imperfection, I have made their future lives easier. I am not setting impossible standards for them. I do not scrutinize my children's grades. I want to know in a general way how they're doing at school. But I don't need to know every last detail about their grades, which ultimately aren't all that important. Nobody really cares what *you* got for your third-quarter English grade when you were in seventh grade, right? So be careful not to push your kids too hard. The world will push them hard enough without your help.

In the Jewish tradition, there is a concept called *pi shnayim,* which means a double portion. According to Jewish law, if there are assets to be divided up after the death of the parents, the oldest child gets a double portion, as a way of compensating him or her for all the mistakes we made as first-time parents. So if they knew 2,500 years ago, when they started to write that stuff down, *that parenting is an imperfect art,* then we moderns can relax, secure in the knowledge that our best efforts, however imperfect, will ultimately yield good people.

Not perfect people. But good enough people. That's because when you're trying to be a father, and when they ultimately will become adults in their own right, the simple truth is that good is good enough.

If I could have one thing back, though, it would be to have learned to manage my temper better. I wish I could travel back in time and recognize that the anger that I displayed to my children was often unnecessary and out of proportion to what tiny mistakes they might have committed. If there's anything more destructive in a home with young children than anger, I don't know what it is.

That's my deepest regret; don't let it be yours.

Discipline Yourself before Disciplining Your Children

To pick up on the thoughts with which I concluded the previous chapter, I truly regret that I spanked my sons when they were little.

I look back and ask myself, what on earth could they have done to deserve that? I remember being spanked by my father, although to be precise, I remember the moment *before* I was spanked. I always wanted to ask my father at that particular moment, "Do you love me?"

My father was old school, and I never had the chance to ask.

The most corrosive thing a father can do is bring his own untreated anger into the house, and that's what happened when I spanked my sons.

I don't regret my alcoholism—I didn't ask for it, and there was a lot about the drinking life that I thoroughly enjoyed. As Joe and Charlie say, alcoholics get to live two lives—the drunken one and the sober one. I made my amends, live differently, and, as the Ninth Step promises say, I don't regret the past.

Except for one glaring thing—I keenly regret those spankings.

This is a chapter about discipline, but before we can talk seriously about how to discipline our children, we really have to have a conversation about how we can best discipline ourselves.

The ultimate lack of discipline for a clean and sober person is to start drinking and using again, but as I heard when I was very new, we are not struck drunk. It's not as though we are taking—and living—the Steps, being sponsored, sponsoring others, going to meetings, reading the literature, asking our Higher Power for help, and suddenly there's a beer in our hand or a line on the mirror and we're off and running.

Slips start long before alcohol and drugs come into the picture. A slip begins the moment we decide that we're going to drink or use when the opportunity presents itself. For most sober people, that moment doesn't present itself often. But when it does, if we have decided to go back to drinking or using, we pick up, simply fulfilling a decision we made days, weeks, or perhaps even months earlier.

It's one thing if you're single, or even married without children. Sure, you'll devastate your parents, siblings, and maybe a few close friends, but if you get drunk or high and throw everything away, or perhaps die, the world will continue to turn. That's not the case when you have children involved.

Looking back, I realize that I know exactly how many of my sober friends' addicted parents died. This one literally drowned in a puddle leaving a bar. That one choked on his own vomit. That one died having sex with his second wife. The next one . . . well, you get the point. Why do I know these things? Because the children of those individuals shared about them, repeatedly, over the years, until the stories were burned into my consciousness.

The Big Book says that we alcoholics are "undisciplined." Before we can even think about how or whether to discipline our children, we have to ask ourselves just how disciplined we are. Are we doing everything that the program asks? Are we processing our emotions with our sponsor, so that we don't take negative feelings into the house? Are we dealing with subtle resentments toward loved ones—perhaps even toward our children—quickly, or are we allowing them to fester and turn into monsters, which eventually turns us into monsters? This isn't idle speculation. As the Big Book says, "The spiritual life is not a theory. We have to live it."

What kind of father walks through the door of your home? Does everybody inside freeze when they hear your key in the lock, wondering what mood you're in, wondering how the evening will go? Or do you contribute to a sense of ease, warmth, and love when you walk in? Are your kids happy to see you? Granted, teens may not show it. But you've got to ask yourself whether you're making the situation better or making it worse.

Are you disciplined to the habit of work? Are you modeling for your children the concept that part of a man's job is to take care of business? Of course women work and should earn as much or more than their spouses or partners. I'm not getting political here. I'm simply saying that we men (as opposed to "guys") have a biological imperative to work, to provide, to be responsible. What about you? Are you meeting your responsibilities to your family (and to your own identity as a man) in this manner?

Are you disciplined in terms of the way you communicate with your partner? That's the number one thing your kids pick up on. Your sons are learning from you how to treat a woman, and your daughters are learning from you how to expect to be treated by a man. If you don't think your actions will have repercussions down the decades for your children, their relationships, and their children, you're just not paying attention. It doesn't take a magician to be a good spouse. Just some kindness and empathy. If you can find that, you'll be fine, and so will they.

What do you do in your spare time? Are you disciplined in your personal habits? What are you modeling for your kids? Most people assume that alcoholism and addiction are genetic traits, a deterministic done deal for your children. But ask yourself this: If it's not entirely genetic, then is it possible that the behavior you model is extremely influential with your kids? To put it more simply, what do you do when you get stressed? Do you panic? Yell? Eat? Withdraw? These are the behaviors your children will one day take on, and probably sooner than later.

Yesterday I was speaking with a business associate who was telling me that her sons had substance issues. All she had, she said, was a glass of wine at night. Well, sometimes all you need is one glass of wine. As we all know, alcoholism and addiction aren't about how much you consumed—it's about where the alcohol or drugs took you. As the expression goes, there are people in my meeting who spilled more than I drank, but I'm still an alkie. It's amazing how forgiving we parents can be of our own foibles and how militaristic we can be about the behavior of our kids.

What do you do in your downtime? Do you get to the gym? Do you have fitness goals? Do you eat in a healthy manner? The problem with food today is that it just tastes so good. A lot of researchers at a lot of food companies make a lot of money figuring out how to make food taste better. As a result, we Americans are ten or fifteen pounds heavier than we were a decade ago. A sober friend of mine in the program who works in a top department store selling men's suits tells me that they actually renumbered suit sizes so men wouldn't feel bad about how heavy they had gotten. A size 42 today was actually a size 46 or 48 not that many years ago. So what kind of example are you setting with regard to diet and exercise for your kids?

And what about rest? The only way I can handle my life is if I get enough sleep. My rest is precious to me, and on nights when I sleep badly, I know that the next day may be rough. Those are days when I especially have to guard my tongue and my actions, around my wife and around my kids. What about you? It's so easy to be up for endless hours, binge watching the latest series on Netflix, online shopping, or just mindlessly surfing the web. It's somewhat hypocritical to be enforcing bedtimes for our kids when we aren't managing to get our own rest. It sounds so crazy, but adequate rest is a determinant of long-term health.

In short, before you even start to think about disciplining your kids, you've got to ask, am I disciplined as a sober member of my Twelve Step program or programs? Am I living my programs? Am I wearing my spirituality like a loose garment, as they say in the rooms, or is that "garment" strangling me or those around me? Am I disciplined as a man, as a spouse or partner, as a worker among workers? And if not, why not?

To put it simply, a disciplined father will find it necessary far less frequently to discipline his kids, because he's already modeling the behavior he wants to see from them.

One of the most important guideposts I have in my role as a father is something I heard from my mentor on parenting, Rabbi Noach Orlowek, an internationally acclaimed Orthodox Jewish parenting expert. Rabbi Orlowek travels the world from his home in Jerusalem, speaking with enormous humility and deep wisdom about being a parent. One of his gems is this:[10] "We are not raising moral children. We are raising children to be moral adults."

In other words, don't be shocked when your precious child lies to you. Children lie. It's what they do. They learn to be honest only when people around them model honesty. Guess what?

So do adults! I wasn't exactly God's gift to honesty when I got to Alcoholics Anonymous. I had to lie about myself, because if you knew the truth, you would hate me as much as I did. In fact, as the AA joke goes, how can you tell if an alcoholic is lying?

His lips are moving.

But it's really amazing how moralistic we formerly immoral people become once we gain the title of parent. Don't be shocked when your kid lies to you. Remember what Rabbi Orlowek says—we are not raising moral children. We are raising children to be moral adults.

Don't be shocked when your child steals something. Learning healthy boundaries is part of what being a kid is all about (if the kid is lucky enough to grow up in a home with healthy boundaries).

I have a college friend who used to say, "My kids will never cry."

Uh, sure.

All I know is that if my expectations of my children are that they will always tell the truth, always do the right thing, and always behave, I'm in for a severe letdown. If I'm not perfect, why am I inflicting my perfectionism on my children?

Kids break things. Kids break things on purpose, to see how strong they are, or because they're angry. They break things by accident because they don't know how strong they are! Kids break things all the time. If I have a collection of Ming vases, I may be somewhat unrealistic if I think that they can coexist with a four-year-old. Maybe it's time to put those Ming vases in storage or just donate them to a museum. Kids break glasses. They drop things. They're careless. You know why? Because they're kids! Here's my solution, and I know that I'm the first person to have thought of this. I call it the $5,000 deductible.

You have an insurance policy on your car, your house, your boat, your health, maybe even your laptop. You've got a deductible on that insurance policy. Well, as soon as my kids were born, they each received a $5,000 lifetime deductible. In other words, the first $5,000 worth of stuff they break—that's on me. After $5,000? Kid, get a job.

Why did I give them a $5,000 deductible? This way, I didn't have to be concerned about them breaking stuff. I didn't have to go into that miserable "now look what you've done" mode. Don't you think a kid feels bad enough if he breaks something? He knows he shouldn't have done that. He might think it's funny on some level, but he knows it's wrong. For a parent to punish an innocent mistake is just plain piling on. For a parent to punish a natural activity relating to a child discovering how big or strong he is, how fast, how agile—that doesn't feel right, either.

There's nothing wrong with having a conversation with the child and letting them know that it's better to be more careful, to respect people's possessions, and also to avoid getting hurt. But punishment? Never once have I gotten on my kids' cases for breaking a dish, a household object of some sort, or anything else.

I'd rather they didn't break things. I will have that conversation with them when these sorts of things happen. But punishment? What's the point? Are you running a family or a penal colony?

Give people a break, even when they break things. Nobody likes a punitive parent. Okay, if it was intentional, that's a different story. Are they modeling your anger? You can't punish your way to a happy home.

The deductible also applies to things kids lose. Kids constantly lose things. That's their job, too. They lose articles of clothing, lunchboxes, baseball mitts, cell phones, caps, and gloves—if it isn't sewn on them, there's a good chance it's not coming home. Deal with it. Just consider the item or items covered by the $5,000 deductible, and you'll find that you aren't breaking your kid's spirit over a sweater that you could replace for $25.

One of the pieces of advice I got when we first started having children, the source of which eludes me, is that "you cannot punish a kid for something you did yourself when you were a kid."

That doesn't give me a lot of leeway, given the fact that when I was a kid I set fire to stuff, including my neighbor's garbage. What if there had been an aerosol can of hair spray in that garbage? Their entire house would've been immolated, and that would've been the end of me, too. I drove like an idiot when I got my license, careening at high speed down the winding streets of my suburban neighborhood, putting myself, my terrified passengers, and any passersby at risk.

I was an idiot.

And this was even before I got into alcohol.

I lied. I called other kids names. I fought. I won "most cooperative" in 1967 at my day camp when I was nine years old, but don't let the fancy camp clothes fool you. I was one of those kids who appeared to be an angel but could act like the devil.

So if I did all that, does that mean I cannot discipline my kids when they get into those sorts of behaviors?

Sometimes I like to say that my role as a parent is similar to that of a flight attendant. I'm here primarily for my kids' safety, and occasionally I toss them a snack.

It's a joke I like to make, but there's actually a lot of truth to it. I am primarily here for their safety. There's physical safety, and then there's feeling safe emotionally. It's my job to promote safety. I always wanted to be on safety patrol when I was a kid. You got the cool belt and the cool medal, and you were allowed to cross other kids at street corners, if memory serves. Well, I'm on the safety patrol now.

Obviously, it means I don't have dangerous objects around the house, and that I keep knives and other things far from the edges of counters where they could fall and cause harm. But if you think of discipline as a means of creating a safe environment—physically safe and emotionally safe—you're probably on the right track.

Rabbi Orlowek, whom I quoted earlier, has another great line. He says that young children are suicidal. In other words, if there's a way to cause themselves harm, they will. Not because they have a death wish but because they're just simply curious, fun loving, and playful (unlike us by this age of our lives!). So it's up to my wife and me to create a safe environment—one where people don't get physically hurt, don't get physically punished, and have a chance to have their feelings acknowledged and honored.

Little children have big feelings. That's why they cry, scream, or shout. They learn control over time, but again, their emotional control is more a function of what I model for them than what I tell them. Remember the Earl Nightingale quote from earlier in the book, "What you're doing speaks so loudly I can hardly hear a word you're saying." In short, the more we discipline ourselves, the less we will likely have to discipline our kids.

There's a lot of debate in the parenting literature about the term *consequences* versus *punishment*. To me, it's a distinction without a difference. If one of my kids does something to another of my kids, there's a consequence, or punishment, or what have you. When my sons were little, they had to go sit on the stairs.

I'm tolerant of most things, but I'm utterly intolerant if one of my children bothers or teases another. I know it happens, and I know it's part of childhood, but that doesn't mean we have to accept it.

The key thing is to partner with your wife on making—and keeping to—the rules, whatever rules you set. Children need consistency—I'll say that over and over because it's so crucial. It doesn't mean you have to enforce every punishment—in my family growing up, we had the concept of "rolling back" punishments if the child's behavior improved. But just make sure the two of you are in accord about what the family rules are and what happens if they are broken.

We also have certain language rules in my home. There are certain words that you are simply not allowed to say. It's a little like in major league baseball—there are certain words that, if you say them to an umpire, will get you tossed. The same thing is true in my home. There are certain words that I find utterly unacceptable. So I don't say them. And I don't let my kids say them. If they do say them, they have to deal with me. (No, not that!!)

The key to effective discipline, I've discovered after years of practicing ineffective discipline, is that the punishment or consequence has to fit the crime, and it has to happen promptly. The longer you go, especially with a small child, between the event and the consequence, the less likely the child is able to learn from the experience. You come back two or three days later and the kid's like, "Are you kidding me? I thought you forgot about this days ago!"

So timeliness and appropriateness are the keys to getting your message across. How quickly? You've got to take enough time so that you can regain your own sense of balance and poise. Quite frankly, you look like a knucklehead to your kid if you give them consequences in the same moment when you're so outraged by their behavior. It's just a recipe for disaster.

Here you are, trying to lecture them against angry behavior, and yet you are ten times angrier than they are. Not a great situation. Doesn't the Big Book say something about pausing when agitated? Well, nothing agitates me like one of my kids bothering, bullying, or teasing another one of my kids or being rude or obnoxious to my wife. I've got to cool off before I barge in.

Do I always? Nope.

Do I make amends afterward? Yup.

Here's another important, practical tip: Never call your child a name. Your child is not stupid, or bad, or thoughtless. Your child's *behavior* might be any of those things. So don't call your kid names, because whatever you say must be true—you're the parent. In one moment of anger, you have hung a label on your kid that he will wear shamefully forever: "I'm stupid." "I'm thoughtless." "I'm an asshole." Why not just get them a tattoo with those words?

So don't label the child; label the behavior and explain what you want.

Unless you really want to see your child develop a dependency on alcohol and drugs to overcome the pain of childhood you inflicted on him or her, don't call your kid names. Along those lines, never use expletives with your children. I've done it on very, very rare occasions, and the guilt ate at me for weeks. The whole world has gone potty-mouth today. Doesn't it make sense for you to make your home a sanctuary where such language is not permitted or tolerated?

So there you are. My thoughts on discipline. Again, it takes a disciplined person to be a good parent, so you want to discipline yourself long before you start thinking about disciplining your kids.

That's the Sober Dad way.

You Can't Always Be Disneyland Dad

As I write these words, I'm reading a hysterical book called *Isn't That Rich?*, a collection of columns by Richard Kirshenbaum about life among the über-rich in Manhattan, where new-money billionaires have trumped old-school millionaires in the social pecking order.[11]

While a lot of the book has to do with money and sex, much of it also has to do with how the super-wealthy raise children or, more accurately, fail to raise them.

There are tales of the author being invited on a Gulfstream G4 . . . by an eleven-year-old.

There are tenth-graders getting bottle service at clubs.

There are drivers, often former cops, tasked with disciplining young miscreants, monitoring their clubbing activities, and making the occasional phone call to a friend on the force in the event that one of these kids has (yet again) broken the law.

It's easy for those of us who do not have a billion-dollar net worth to scoff at such horrific parenting. The reality is that while, as F. Scott Fitzgerald wrote in his short story "The Rich Boy," "They [the rich] are different from you and me," when it comes to failing to set healthy limits, we can be just as bad as the One Percent.

So let's spend some time thinking about what it means for undisciplined alcoholics and addicts to set limits for our kids. What do we need to limit, why do we need to do it, and how do we get it done?

Our culture today does not really benefit kids. If you would like to nominate that sentence for understatement of the century, I will happily accept the honor. All the things that we thought were great when we were teens—access to sex and drugs, limited parental supervision, sex and violence in the movies and on videos—don't look quite as appealing now that we're the parents. I grew up in the 1970s, no one's idea of a naïve time. And yet, I managed to find my way into, and most of the time out of, a lot of trouble. So there's a certain irony in sober fathers, who may well have been the worst hell-raisers on the planet, no strangers to anonymous sex, incarceration, or even anonymous *sex during* incarceration, sitting and fretting over whether a particular PG-13 movie is inappropriate for his little darlings. But you know what? That's life. That's where we are now, thank you God, and that's our job.

When I accompany my teenage sons to the movies, I sit there and marvel, but not in a good way, over who exactly decided that a particular movie was PG-13. I know the PG stands for parental guidance, but exactly which parents are we consulting? I know that we're talking about family values, but sometimes it seems like the family in question are the Mansons. I took one son to see *Divergent,* which I can only compare to what home movies of the Holocaust might have looked like. I don't know if I would've felt less awkward and uncomfortable had the entire cast taken off all its clothes and indulged in group sex. The movie was shockingly, stunningly violent, and it was good ol' PG-13. How can this be?

I've mentioned that I lived in Los Angeles for many years and got sober there. Because of my non-anonymous writing career, I did a fair amount of work with people in Hollywood. Individually, they may be quite nice. Collectively, however, these are the *last* people on earth you want raising your kids. And yet, the standards they set, the cultural race to the bottom that they inflict on our families, goes on unabated. It's just unfortunate.

Michael Medved wrote a book called *Hollywood vs. America,*[12] in which he made the same point—it's almost as though our culture is purposefully seeking to destroy the moral fiber of our kids (and our adults). In that excellent book, Medved, a top radio talk show host and movie critic, destroys Hollywood's argument that "if we make clean movies, nobody wants to come see them."

The opposite is true. *Forrest Gump,* a fairly clean movie, grossed a gazillion dollars. *Frozen*? Even more. If you build it, they will come. Look at the Pixar films, which are a blessing to parents. I can tell you as a parent that if I get wind of an age-appropriate movie in which nobody strips and nobody dies, I cannot wait to rush my kids to the theater to see it. I will wait in the lobby with my eight-year-old until the previews have finished, because for every one movie that's somewhat decent, you've got nine or ten more that are violent or otherwise inappropriate. What's a father to do?

Setting limits, however, isn't something that starts when your kids become old enough to clamor for PG-13 films (or sneak off to see them without your knowledge). It starts from the earliest ages. Your job is to deal with this moving target of where exactly the limits should be set, while finding the sweet spot between compulsively overcontrolling your children and being overly lax.

There's a little Disneyland dad in all of us, the aspect of our nature that wants to let our kids have ice cream for breakfast and stay up all night playing video games, because then, we believe, they will love us.

It's not exactly love. It isn't respect, either. The biggest issue in our home, from the infancy of our children through the present day, has to do with limits on screen time. What are they watching, and how long are they watching it for? I'll share with you some of the things that have worked for us.

The default mode for parenting is to stick your kid in front of a television screen or computer screen and just leave them there, for as many hours as it takes. This is low-engagement, low-reward parenting at its worst. The best term for screens, whether they are TV, desktop, laptop, tablet, smartphone, or anything in between, is the *one-eyed babysitter.* Here's the problem. Research* indicates that babies' brains aren't formed enough even until they're two years old to absorb the stimulation of video without some negative effect on their development. Is this what you want for your kid?

I know that you and your partner are both exhausted from work, sleeplessness, parenting, and the rest. But at the same time, plopping goggle-eyed Junior in front of the widescreen is the worst thing you can do for him. I hate to say this, but now that you went to all the trouble of having a kid (I know—for you it wasn't that much trouble at all), you have to play with him or her.

In his book *Babyhood,* Paul Reiser[13] writes that his wife left him alone with their two-year-old son for an hour and said, "Just play with him." Reiser says that they did puzzles, played

---

* Please don't ask me what research. I just sound so smart when I get to say "research indicates"—even if I made the "research" up.

with blocks, read a book, drew, and did a couple of other activities. When Reiser looked to see if the hour had gone by, he realized that only five minutes had passed.

I know you're a hard-charging, type A, make-up-for-lost-time alcoholic or addict. I know, I truly know that by playing with your kid, you're missing out on the opportunity to respond to thirty more emails and texts or watch the latest episode of *Homeland*. "Look, Daddy has a screen, and baby has a screen!" No. That's just not going to work. Not for the kind of kid you want to raise.

So the first limit you have to set is on yourself, to not give your child the option to sit passively and be overstimulated by all those colors, lights, and sounds. Even *Club Penguin* is like Vegas for six-year-olds. There have to be some restrictions on time. Otherwise, your kid will happily sit there for hours, motionless, allowing you to tear through those life-changing emails and texts or catch up on Facebook. (Hey, Sober Dad's on Facebook—come hang out with me!*) But those lost moments will never come back. Spend them with your child. They'll never be this young again.

Along these lines, I want to pass along a suggestion from the master motivator Tony Robbins, who points out that life is a series of great moments, and it's our job as parents to create great moments for our young children. He suggests that you should open up a file on your laptop called Magic Moments.

Then, whenever your child does or says anything sweet or funny, or if you go on a day trip somewhere, or spend time with another relative, whatever it is, write it down immediately in that file. Otherwise, as he says, the event goes right down

---

* But only when your kids are asleep.

the memory hole, and you end up like the rest of the parents who say to themselves, "The first five years" (or "the first fifteen years") "were an absolute blur."

I heard Robbins present that idea about the Magic Moments file eleven years ago, and as a result, we have a seventeen-page, single-spaced, growing list of many of the most delectable moments of our four kids' childhoods. Occasionally I back the file up to Google Drive, or email it around to family members. Sometimes the kids will all crowd around on the couch and we will just read through the list and remember stuff and laugh together. They feel enormous joy, I believe, over the fact that someone cared enough about them to write all this stuff down. It's something special in all of our lives.

So run, don't walk, to your laptop, start that Magic Moments file, put down all the Greatest Hits that you can recall, and then keep adding to it as time goes on. One day, you and your children will thank you.

We very carefully handpicked the videos our kids could watch when they were little. We were big on *Teletubbies,* because it's so innocent. (I actually enjoy watching it when I'm doing a long run on the treadmill at the gym, but that's probably a story for another day.*) We were not big *Barney* fans. To me, those kids are just a little too well-scrubbed. I just found those videos to be, well, icky. Just one man's opinion. The kids in *Teletubbies,* by contrast, when they go to those videos that pop up on the Teletubbies' tummies, are working-class English kids who look real. Somehow that seemed smarter.

Too much information about Teletubbies? Sorry.

I admit we fell for the Baby Einstein stuff. The idea is that if you play classical music for your kid, he'll be smarter. Of

---

* When my therapist, who vetted the manuscript, saw this line, she put in a note that said, "See me."

course, the Baby Einstein videos are simply extended video toy catalog ads. My children didn't learn a lot about Mozart from Baby Einstein, but they sure learned a lot about "I want *that*!"

When our first child was about a year old, she developed a habit of waking up very early—around 5:00 or 5:30. I'm an early riser, so it didn't really cause a problem for me, other than the fact that I was now spending my quiet time watching my daughter's favorite video with her over and over.

I described my dilemma to a spiritually minded civilian friend (a civilian is someone who is neither an alcoholic nor an addict). I wanted to meditate in the morning, but my daughter wanted to watch that video.

"Watching that video *is* your meditation now," he said, neatly solving the problem.

As the kids got a little older, we made a decision that they could not watch anything with human faces, or sitcoms aimed at kids. Pretty much all sitcoms for children boil down to one idea: Adults are absolute freaking idiots. The message is reinforced in a thousand ways: Teachers and principals are dorks. Parents are dorks. All adults, and especially all authorities, in fact, are dorks. The only people in the world who have common sense are good-looking eleven-year-olds, so they should in fact have all the power.*

The show we had the most trouble with was the Disney sitcom *The Suite Life of Zack and Cody*. In these shows, and many others, you never even saw adults. The message is that if you don't see adults, then you just don't need them. And if you don't need them, it becomes much harder for real adults—you and me, for example—to be heard when we have important things to say.

---

* Although maybe if they ran the government, it wouldn't be much worse than what we've got right now. Who's with me on this one?

We're big on *Phineas and Ferb,* and I confess I allow my thirteen-year-olds to watch *Futurama,* hoping that they don't get all the jokes. The other smart move we made was to buy boxed sets of *I Love Lucy* episodes. It's amazing how well those shows hold up. If your kid has to watch something, give them a taste of genuine 1950s black and white.

As you get to know your kids' friends, get to know their parents. Find some go-to people who have the same values you do instead of trying to go it alone. See what they're letting their kids watch and listen to. See what limits they're setting. As they say in Al-Anon, reason things out. There are a lot of great websites that rate movies for kids or aggregate the ratings of parents, but who are those parents, exactly? Do we know what their values are? Are they trying to raise the same kind of kids you are? I'm not here to tell you what limits to set. I am saying that you want to determine what lines you want to draw, and then stick to them.

Let's talk about phones. Delay, delay, delay getting your kid a smartphone. I know all the other kids have iPhones and Androids. I know your kid will despise you—and by extension me, if you show them this book—for not giving them the latest and greatest smartphone. In reality, it's too much access—too much porn, too much violence, too much time playing games— and they can't handle it. Actually, most adults can't limit their own screen time, so how do you expect your kids to do so?

Do not put the whole world in their pocket.

Get them a dumb phone—one that calls and texts and tells them the time (as in, you're supposed to be home by now).

If they don't want a dumb phone, then they get no phone at all.

Parents today are so isolated from each other—how ironic that we have the greatest communication tools in the history of mankind, and yet when was the last time you had an actual, real, live friend (as opposed to a Facebook friend) in your home? We're just too busy. What exactly we're doing, I'm not sure, but we sure are busy doing it.

Setting limits also has to do with bedtime and other routines. Mornings and evenings can be havoc unless you adopt and stick to a routine that works for you and your kids. Children need consistency. They need to get up and go to sleep at roughly the same time every day. They need to get in the habit of having their clothing ready at night for the next morning, their dirty clothing in the hamper, their teeth brushed and flossed, and, when they are of school age, their bags or backpacks ready the night before. If your child is scrambling every morning to get stuff together, it's not because the child is disorganized. *You* are, and you are training your child to be equally disorganized.

Even if you have never had an organized moment in your life, it's time to start figuring out how to make a plan to keep the trains running on time. It's really not that complicated. Make a list of what your kid needs to do to get out the door in the morning and a separate list for what your kid needs to do to get to bed.

They should go to bed at roughly the same time every night, unless there's a big family outing or holiday. They should get up at the same time every morning. Get them into their routines. Routines create a sense of security. Alcoholics and addicts believe that rules are for other people. Unfortunately, now that you are sober, you are one of those other people, and so are your kids!

They may not thank you for the fact that every night at 8:00 all electronics go off, snacks get done for the next morning, showers and baths are taken, teeth are brushed and flossed, and so on. But they'll grow up to be organized, efficient people.

You'll also benefit by avoiding the brain damage that comes from having one or more kids scrambling around to get out the door in the morning because homework is undone, lunch is missing, snacks aren't packed, and so on. And you won't have kids bleary-eyed and snapping at you at the breakfast table because they were up way too late watching Madden Mobile videos. Again.

Okay, that's enough on routines. Establish them early, and they will serve you well. I mentioned earlier that one of our favorite routines is reading to our kids at night, something we've done since before they were old enough to understand words. They certainly understood love and attention, though, and that's what reading to your kids provides. I know I've mentioned this before, but it's well worth reiterating—the best way to get kids off to dreamland is to lie down with them in bed and read them a nice book. Before you know it, you might be conking out too. Will this interfere with your sex life? Absolutely.

The Disneyland dad wants to be his kids' best friend, and that's not what they need. In *The Blessing of a Skinned Knee*,[14] psychologist Dr. Wendy Mogel writes about the high priest in the temple in Jerusalem who would wear an elaborate outfit described in painstaking detail in the book of Leviticus. Why did the high priest wear this outfit? she asks. It's because the experience of putting on all those priestly garments transformed not only the high priest but also those around him.

It changed his whole picture of himself, no doubt, and reminded him of the seriousness of the task of atoning for the entire nation of Israel on Yom Kippur. At the same time, all of the priests who saw the high priest in this outfit had to be struck themselves by the gravitas of the moment and probably sat up a little straighter in their chairs. They no doubt took the whole experience more seriously, seeing him all dressed up this way.

Her point is that a generation or two ago, men dressed like men. They wore a jacket and tie, even to the ball game. There was a dignity to the way they appeared. That dignity had an effect on the rest of the family. Take a look at those episodes of *Father Knows Best,* where you see Robert Young in a jacket and tie. Mogel suggests that something important is lost in today's world, where the father dresses like an older brother. Again, we men aren't owning our manhood. It's confusing to children. We need to put on our own high priest outfits, whatever they might look like in today's world. We need to act like leaders, or co-leaders, in the family, instead of the Peter Pan–like world's oldest teenager mode of dressing that so many men unthinkingly adopt. It's up to us to set the tone.

I said in the previous chapter that we have to learn how to discipline ourselves before we can even think about providing discipline for our children. The same thing is true here. If we want to set limits for our children, let's first learn to set them for ourselves. Let's look, act, and even dress like adults. As my sponsor says, if you look like an adult, and you sound like an adult, and you work like an adult, and you do all the things adults do, eventually, people will start to mistake you for an adult!

I would rather our children mistakenly assume that we are adults than all-too-accurately realize that we are only slightly larger versions of *them.*

Limits create a sense of security for children. It's our job to provide healthy limits, consistent routines, and above all, endless, endless love.

Labels Belong on Clothes, Not Kids

Before I got married, I took a marriage class that consisted of sitting opposite the class's instructor, an insurance executive, in his office, one-on-one for about four hours. Some of the advice he gave in that class can be found in the pages of this book. One of the most important things he said, as I touched on earlier, was that a wife's self-esteem is dependent to a very large degree on the way her husband speaks about her, in her presence and with others.

The same thing is true of your child.

We parents forget just how huge we are, physically and in every other way, in the eyes of our children. Whatever we say about them must be true. So it is incredibly important to recognize the power we have to build or destroy their self-worth with the words we speak about them and the words we allow others to use about them as well.

As I mentioned earlier, labels are for shirts, not children. Never, ever think you're being cute, clever, or helpful when you give your children labels, as in, "She's the smart one," "He's the athletic one," or "He's the troublemaker."

It's so unfair. Sometimes parents do this as a way of punishing their children for behavior that they otherwise cannot control, as in, "Since you keep on causing me so much trouble, I'm going to tell the world what a jerk you are."

Thanks, Dad.

These definitions are usually delivered with a knowing smile, as if the other adult is in on the conspiracy about what a good or bad child this particular child is. Why don't you just put the child in foster care right now, instead of inflicting any more damage yourself? Children are not likely to appreciate the labels, but they will believe them. These definitions often condemn the child for a behavior that the child may well have learned from watching his parents (gotcha!). Or maybe the behavior is a cry for help that the parents are too self-centered to notice.

A positive label can be just as dangerous and harmful as a negative one. Living up to the burden of "the smart one" or "the well-behaved one" denies a child the right to a full range of behaviors and attitudes. In other words, you're pigeonholing people before they've had a chance to discover who they really are. Ever wonder why alcoholics and addicts are such black-and-white thinkers? Maybe because they grew up in homes where everything was either really great or really horrible, including themselves.

Why parents go on hurting their kids this way is beyond me, but please recognize that there is a price to be paid. The AA cliché rings true: Hurt people hurt people. The ultimate booby prize for hurtful parenting is a child who translates into addiction the emotional pain his parents dealt out. Don't go blaming genetics when you set your kid up to be miserable because of the way you spoke to him or the way you spoke *about* him. You've got to own it.

One of my favorite lessons in parenting came from Cal Ripken Sr., father of Cal Ripken Jr., the player who holds the record for most consecutive major league games played, and two other brothers, one of whom was also a decent major leaguer in his own right, but certainly not a legend like Cal Jr. I remember seeing the father interviewed on TV. "You must be proud of Cal Jr.," the interviewer gushed.

Cal Sr. calmly replied, "We're proud of all of our children."

Perfect.

If one of your children receives a compliment in the presence of the other children, don't assume that the other children have the maturity to take it as anything less than an insult to them, especially if they are young. Children buy into the idea that there are roles to be played in families. If Sally is the smart one, they reason, I must be the dumb one. Or if Fred is well-behaved, then I'm going to stake out the territory of the kid who always screws up. Maybe you made a decision along these lines yourself when you were a kid, based on the behavior of your siblings or the labels of your parents.

Birth order matters.

First children (myself included) tend to be the most serious and fearful, because our parents are terrified of making mistakes and put us on a path toward overly serious views of life. Middle children often struggle to determine where they fit in. They knew they were the younger child until an even younger one came along. They had an identity, but they lost it suddenly. No wonder they resent their baby brother or sister—not only do they get all the attention, but now that one is the "baby of the family." That's not fair!

Younger children are often the happiest and most relaxed, because by now, the parents have developed some self-confidence in their roles. They also have a wealth of role models from which to choose, sometimes for better or worse, in terms of their parents and older siblings. I was once at a John Bradshaw five-day seminar on parenting when I was fairly new in sobriety. I was sitting in the front row, taking notes like crazy. When he got to talking about birth order, he said, "First children take the most notes." Our eyes met, but my pen never left the page. We knew.

My wife and I have twins, as I've mentioned. They were born twins, and twins they will always be, with a unique bond that the rest of us who are mere singletons will never fully understand. I just wish that when adults, who presumably should know better, encounter twins, they don't have to go through the same dumb litany of statements like, "You guys look alike!"

Or "How can I tell you apart?"

Or "Do you guys ever fool your teachers?"

Once and for all: Hahaha. So funny.

For a while, I tried to tell people that my boys had been born twins, but now they were just brothers. Unfortunately, my remedy for the situation evinced so much eye rolling from my sons that I gave up with it. Twins are fascinating, but if you come upon any, try to treat them as individuals and not as a vaudeville act. Everyone will be happier.

Why? Because twins, especially identical twins, struggle to establish independent identities. How could I be a unique person in the world, they wonder, if there is someone who looks so much like me right here? Twins don't like getting lumped together. They can feel enmeshed. They want to be understood as their own person. And if you upset one of my sons, they will both beat the stuffing out of you. Which is as it should be.

I have to take a moment to acknowledge Tim Kurkjian, the baseball authority on ESPN. Through my work, I was able to bring my sons for a tour of the ESPN studios, and they met many of the on-air personalities, including Kurkjian. He looked up from his preparations for his next on-air appearance and studied my sons carefully, looking back and forth at them before he spoke.

"You are twins," he said finally. "But there really are differences in the way you look. If people take the time, they'll see them."

I could have kissed him, but that would have required a lot of explaining to my sons. Here was someone who was acknowledging two individuals, typically lumped together into one dumb joke, for what they were: two individuals. Why can't everybody do that?

I try very hard never to criticize my children in front of each other or in front of relatives, friends, or even strangers. It's awful when parents turn passersby into participants in their own family psychodrama. *Hey,* I want to tell them. *Discipline your own kid on your own time, but don't bring me into it. I'm not here to serve as an audience for your histrionics. It's hard enough for any of us to receive criticism. To do it in front of an audience of strangers is just plain cruel. If you have to say something negative to your child, take him or her aside where no one else can hear, say what you need to say, and move on.*

The other question you have to answer for yourself is just how often you're going to criticize or punish your child for various infractions, and you've also got to decide at what point you're going to inject yourself into situations involving your kids. We know a family whose attitude toward parenting is punitive to a cringe-worthy degree. From the time their kids were little—and these are good kids—they had been subjected to a barrage of criticism for every little ticky-tack thing that a kid could do wrong. How do we know this? Because the parents never stop, even with us in the room. They just hammer at those kids. It's just wrong. Children have to have a certain amount of freedom to be imperfect, or they're going to end up in Twelve Step programs themselves (if they're lucky), talking about how they're such perfectionists but can't figure out why.

Rather than hammer your kid for every single possible misstep, the wiser course is to decide on a few lines in the sand and then try to let everything else go, or, if you must say something, just make it a brief comment as opposed to a whole speech.

For me, as I've said, the lines in the sand have to do with using swear words, teasing or bullying another family member, or being (overly) rude to myself and my wife. Anything else, I might say something or I might not, but the kids already know how I feel. It all comes back to my core guidepost—*we're not raising moral children; we are raising children to be moral adults.* I don't expect them to tell me the truth all the time. I don't expect them to keep their rooms perfectly clean. I don't expect them to get A-plusses. All I want them to do is show up, behave decently, treat each other and us decently, and get on with their day.

I'm no tiger mom or tiger dad; I think you can figure that one out. But by the same token, I will not tolerate the things I will not tolerate—bad language, bullying, teasing, or destruction of property. Those are my rules; make your own, but don't make everything a violation that sends the kid to the penalty box.

For me, the best example of behavior modification that I can offer a first-time dad is the relationship between players and referees in the NBA. One of the great referees of all time, Mendy Rudolph, had a great expression: To be a great referee, you had to "swallow the whistle." Let 'em play. That's what the fans want to see. They want the athletes to be able to get into a flow and make the game fun and worth watching. That's exactly the same thing I've tried to do with my kids—swallow the whistle and let them play. I don't want to be the ref who gets a reputation for having a red you-know-what and always tossing people. Am I operating out of an unhealthy desire to be liked instead of respected? No. It's just that I would rather be respected than feared. Am I making sense?

Tim Donaghy, the NBA referee who became infamous for giving information about betting lines to the mafia, tells a fascinating story in his memoir, *Personal Foul*.[15] He says the very first game he refereed was in Philadelphia, as the 76ers were taking on Michael Jordan's Bulls. Midway through the first period, Donaghy called a foul on Jordan. To the newbie referee's shock, the entire Philadelphia crowd started booing him lustily.

Jordan and his legendary coach, Phil Jackson, came striding over to Donaghy to ask what he was thinking. Donaghy suddenly realized that he wasn't there to call a foul on every single play that merited a foul, especially if it involved the great Michael Jordan. Fans don't come to see the referees—they come to see the players. By the same token, children don't want referees for parents—they want parents for parents.

At the same time, I try to insert myself into situations before they turn into full-fledged arguments or worse. If I hear raised voices from a bedroom, I'll go knock on the door and ask, like the friendly cop on the beat, "Everything okay in there?"

They know what's behind that question. They know that it's a warning that if they don't settle down, they'll both face consequences for whatever happens next, and I'm not going to sit there and listen to two sides and adjudicate.

Sometimes, after a heated situation with a sibling, a child just wants to be heard. Sometimes I have the patience, and honestly, sometimes I don't. The easiest way for my kids to avoid dealing with me when I'm deeply annoyed is to avoid having a situation begin in the first place. I think that's a good lesson for kids.

Years ago, a newspaper columnist named Erma Bombeck wrote fantastic articles, collected in books which you can probably find on Amazon for a penny, about family matters. My favorite column[16] talked about how when she was growing up, her father was a distant figure, one that she and her siblings never really knew all that well. When he came home from work, he might sit and have a drink while reading the newspaper and waiting for dinner. If there was discipline to be doled out, he did it. When he took his seat at the head of the dinner table, the kids didn't misbehave. They didn't dare.

Bombeck wrote that in today's world, children have a much more relaxed view of their fathers. Sometimes the father cultivates an air of being an older brother instead of the old man. Bombeck's surprising conclusion: Maybe something was lost when families lost that imperious head of the household whom the children did not know all that well.

It's a fascinating point to debate, and I am certainly not about to advocate, or become, the kind of father Bombeck had. And yet, just as I was never allowed to sit in my grandfather's chair, while he was alive or after he passed, my children are not allowed to sit in my chair. Sometimes, when we have a guest—a clergyman or some other individual whom I want my kids to understand that I respect deeply, I will have him sit in my chair. I don't have to say a word to my kids. They get the message.

The whole point of speaking well of your kids, and speaking respectfully to them, and taking that Mendy Rudolph approach of swallowing the whistle and letting them play, is to increase the likelihood that you're going to have a relatively happy home. Kids will always test your boundaries. It's like the Macaulay Culkin line in *Uncle Buck*—that's my job.

The job of refereeing in a broad sense—watching their behavior and choosing when and how to intervene—doesn't end until they're out of the home. It just seems to go on forever, especially when they are teens. But kids get there. They get there at their own pace, and in their own fashion, and ultimately they decide where "there" is.

It always astonishes me in today's world when parents are clearly seeking to live their own thwarted dreams through their children, directing them toward sports that the kids may not want to play, extracurricular activities that do not call out to the child, or even careers that the kids feel no calling toward. As God is my judge, if zero of my four kids become professional writers, I could care less. Unless it's what *they* want.

Do I have goals for them? Absolutely. I want them to be happy. I am not responsible for their happiness, but I must not be responsible for creating misery for them. Happiness ultimately is a choice they must make for themselves. They have to determine what gives them joy and what they believe is worth working toward. They get to define their own pursuit of happiness. My job is to model happiness and also to help them with coping tools when unhappy events, small or large, occur.

My next goal: I want them to contribute to society in any way they choose—I don't want them just to be takers. I want them to create homes of their own and raise good kids. What they do for a career, or what education path they take to get there, or what extracurricular activities they favor, or what sports they play . . . it's none of my business. It is in the sense that I have to pay for it and drive them there, but beyond that? It's up to them. Sure, they're my kids, but they're God's kids, too, and above all, they are their own people.

Rabbi Orlowek has another great line: He says, "Parenting is an orderly transfer of power from the parent to the child." I love that. That's also been one of my major guideposts throughout my career as a dad. I want them to enjoy all the power that's appropriate for their age, stage, and level of maturity. I don't want to give them so much power that I'm potentially harming them, and I don't want them to feel so powerless that they end up emotionally crippled.

It's not an exact science, but the main thing I want them to know is that life is about making choices and accepting the consequences, good or bad, that arise from those choices. It's only through making choices that we actually learn something.

I agree with Tony Robbins that it's up to each of us to define success and failure in terms that empower us. For me, success equals "going for it" and failure equals "not going for it." In my business, I try a lot of things, most of which don't work. But the things that do work, sometimes work spectacularly.

I like what legendary UCLA basketball coach John Wooden says: "The team that makes the most mistakes wins." I let my kids make mistakes, and I don't criticize them for making mistakes. I applaud them for going for it in whatever area they choose. That's what life is—making choices and seeing what happens. If I deny them the right to make choices, or if I criticize heavily the choices they make, they will become cowardly, afraid of life, unable to function. That's not what I want.

What I want for my kids boils down to this: Because of my incipient alcoholism and all the untreated emotional pain I lived with, coming out of an alcoholic, divorced home, not too many years after I graduated college, I hit the ground. I want my kids to be able to hit the ground running. Where they go, how far and how fast, is up to them. My job as a parent is simply to facilitate that orderly transfer of power and let them fly.

So be very careful with the words you use when you speak to your children, and be equally careful with the words—and especially the labels—you use when you speak about them. Their self-worth is in your hands, or more accurately, on your tongue. Say the right thing, do the right thing, and let them play.

Don't Hesitate to Reward for Good Behavior and Good Grades

Should you pay your kid to get A's? Absolutely.

I remember a long time ago seeing a cartoon in *The New Yorker* magazine. Two young mothers were pushing strollers in Central Park. One said to the other, peering into her friend's stroller, "How are his grades?"

The pressure parents place on their children to succeed in school, just about everywhere, is nightmarish. The whole system is absurd. So let's step back and ask, what do we really expect our kids to do in school? What do we have to encourage them to do, and what do we need to protect them from? That's what we'll examine in this chapter.

Alcoholics and addicts typically have two types of parents—perfectionists and drunks. The perfectionists are wondering why you only got a 98 instead of 100 on your exam. The drunk couldn't care less and doesn't even know what grade you're in.

As a result, we end up with these competing voices in our heads—do your best, but it doesn't really matter, because nothing matters. We oscillate between nihilism and a sense of intensity that the outcome of the Free World is a function of our grade point average. And now we try to parent *our* kids, with these voices battling it out in our brains.

So what does a sober dad do?

I would love my kids to succeed royally at whatever they do. I want them to get the highest grades in the history of humanity. I want them to have fulfilling careers that make them a ton of money, have great relationships with their spouses, and present me with numerous grandchildren, all of whom are just as fabulous as their parents.

But what do I really want for them?

As I said in the previous chapter, I want them to be happy.

Our society confuses what Tony Robbins calls "means goals" and "end goals." An end goal is what we really want. For me, the *end* goal with my kids is (all together now) I want them to be happy. The *means* goal is the best idea I have in order to achieve the end goal I've set forth. In our society, we place far too much emphasis on the means goals: Make a million dollars. Have a hot girlfriend. Whatever. And then we either neglect the end goals, or we never even articulate exactly what we're hustling around trying to do.

And then we pass on this same imperfect mentality to our children. We want them to do all these things, but we never help them establish what their real end goals should be.

I'm not talking about taking out a sheet of paper with your kids and having them write down their three-year, five-year, and ten-year goals. Instead, the best thing we can do for our kids is to model happiness, to model balance, and to model any other end goal that we have created for ourselves. Then, we are able to put the means by which we seek to reach those goals into perspective. And that brings us back to the question of education. Why do you want your kid to do well in school? So that you'll look good? So that you can feel smart and hold your head up high when you're talking with other parents? Or is it because if they do well in school, certain doors will open up to them, they will be able to pursue certain careers that will bring them happiness and fulfillment, and so on. In other words, before you start creating expectations for your kids, ask yourself what expectations you've created for yourself and whether you are living up to them or not. We don't want to be the pathetic parent who is living out academic, financial, athletic, or artistic goals through our children when we never really figured out what we wanted for ourselves.

This is a very long way of saying that grades are important, but you've got to stop and ask yourself, why am I insisting on my kids working hard in school? What do I hope they will gain? And how do I not allow my alcoholism or addiction to turn them into "human doings." What's a "human doing"? Someone who's on autopilot, careening from event to event, and typically messing everything up along the way. What does the Big Book say? "Sweet relationships are dead. Affections have been uprooted. Selfish and inconsiderable habits have kept the home in turmoil."[17] And one's work life isn't much better.

Thus the "joke," except it isn't really a joke: What do you call a practicing alcoholic or addict without a girlfriend?

Homeless.

So "human doings" are totally out of touch with their feelings and just simply consumed with grades, extracurricular activities, and college applications, or if they're older, money, work, and sex.

The question thus becomes: How do I live my life so that my kids will have the most fulfilling lives for themselves?

I don't know who invented homework, but I propose that we get a few of us together, find the guy, take him into an alley, and beat the crap out of him. Homework is the dumbest thing in the world. Everything that they tell adults about time management, which is really emotion management, has to do with work-life balance. Nobody applauds a parent who works a long day at the office, comes home, turns on his laptop, and goes back to work. And yet, the whole homework nightmare involves pushing kids to spend what free time they have in an unbalanced struggle to get better grades than the next kid.

Actually, that's not entirely accurate. Parents put inordinate pressure on their children in order to succeed in school, but at the same time, the schools are under unbelievable pressure to have high test scores. The jobs of administrators hang in the balance. Budgets rise and fall depending on what kind of standardized test numbers a school can generate. Teachers have virtually no flexibility in terms of what they can present in the classroom, because they are under a mandate to teach in a manner that will get the school's standardized test scores as high as possible. In other words, your kid is working overtime to save the jobs of his school's administrators. That's why I say homework is dumb.

For years, when my children were small and I thought they had too much homework, I would do a lot of it for them. If I thought the assignment size was excessive, I might have them do one math problem and I would do the next, or they would do one page and I would do a page or two—anything to get through it. I actually confessed this to the principal of my kids' school, and he admitted that he did exactly the same thing!

I admit this might not have been the best idea, and I see the value of not undermining the authority of teachers and administrators. But back then, it was all I could think of to solve a vexing problem. I said I was Sober Dad, not Perfect Dad.

The system is fundamentally broken. Most schoolteachers are extremely dedicated and hardworking. Others go into the field because of two words—July and August. Some schools are well-managed, and some are poorly run; some years, your kids will have great teachers and some years, not so much. So the question is this: As a parent, what's your role? How much do you add to the pressure your child is already facing? And is there any way out of a system that isn't truly geared to put the needs of the students first?

No parent needs to be reminded about the perilous state of the economy. Parents are rightly concerned that if their children do not succeed in school, they will fail at the "big sort" that determines which students go to which colleges. A degree from a top college is a gateway to the highest socio-economic levels of American society, while many parents interpret a diploma from a lesser school as a ticket to economic uncertainty.

Let's dispel that myth quickly. I have worked for many individuals with a net worth exceeding $100 million, and three of my clients are bona fide billionaires. Of them, not a single one graduated from an Ivy League school. They went to state colleges or mediocre private colleges, or had no college at all. You can show me all the economic data you want indicating that a college degree that costs a quarter of a million dollars or more is worth more than a degree that costs one fifth as much. But I know the net worths of my clients. I know their educational histories. And I need to tell you that some people I know made vast fortunes without ever setting foot in the Ivy League or any school of that caliber.

I've taught college. I taught at a well-regarded but certainly not top-dog private college in the Boston area. The pressure students are under to get great grades, to have extraordinary extracurricular activities on their CVs, to have great recommendations—it's absurd. I've seen this firsthand. We are training children to grow up to be miserable, careerist adults.

Out of the sixty students I taught over two years, maybe only one should have even been in college. The rest should have been starting their working lives, or just simply getting married and having families. They weren't smart enough to benefit from the kind of independent thinking that a college education is supposed to foster. Let me rephrase that. They might have been smart, but not book smart. So why do parents shove books down these kids' throats?

Most of the students at this particular college came from families in which they were the first generation to go to college. Their parents—typically their fathers—were small-business people with high school educations. I sensed, although I have no proof, that many of them sent their offspring to college either because it's what they were told to do or because there was a certain amount of bragging rights to be gained by telling their friends that their kid went to such and such college. But did it do the kid any good?

This was twenty years ago, long before the American attention span was shredded by social media, texting, and other forms of technology. Back then, people still had brains in their heads. And yet, I never fully escaped the awkward feeling that I was lecturing to an empty classroom even though every seat was taken.

If you want to succeed at anything, start with the goal in mind and work backward. What do you want for your kids? You want them to be economically self-sufficient. You want them to have adequate credentials to get the jobs they desire. You don't want them coming back and living in your basement, poking around the fridge, and walking in on what should have been your empty-nester magic moments with your wife.

How best do you avoid this "failure to launch?"

America is a much more egalitarian society than practically anywhere else on earth. It really doesn't matter where you come from. It does matter how hard you work. I have a client right now who had no college and made millions starting a moving company after the guys who moved him did the typically crappy job that movers do. It's not as though a college degree is a winning Powerball ticket printed on sheepskin. It's a tool, and a very expensive one. So if you're looking for your children to become economically self-sufficient, you have to ask whether loading them up with debt is the best way to make that happen. Reasonable minds may differ.

So first you've got to decide whether your desire to have your child in college, or in a top college, is a function of economic necessity or a display of your own ego. I have lived in three American cities where people in those cities all worshipped the same thing. In LA, it's fame. In Boston, it's educational attainment. In New York, it's wealth. I have yet to meet an individual for whom fame, illustrious educational attainment, or net worth in and of itself translated into either a happy or meaningful life.

I'm not opposed to education. I'm just saying that maybe we put too much stress on it, and therefore maybe we put too much stress into our children's lives. Whatever you're going to do, ask yourself, is this really best for my kid?

In Lake Wobegon, Garrison Keillor says that all the children are "above average." I'm not suggesting that you brand your kid as too stupid for college. I am saying that forcing your child into the misery of competing with his classmates and friends for grades, SAT scores, internships, and the rest of it may be a path to economic success, but it certainly is not the road to happiness. And if your children attend institutions, public or private, where there's simply too much homework and not enough chance for the kids to develop in other ways, maybe this isn't a case of one size fits all.

This is a long, perhaps overly long, way of saying that you

want to think twice before you add to the already enormous pressure your child faces. Today, it's commonplace for high school students to be so exhausted from the chase for grades and college acceptances that by the time they get to college, they are too burned out to benefit from the experience. Yes, they won—they made it into a top school. But they simply cannot crank up the machinery once again and go through yet another chase for grades and recommendations and internships, this time in search of admission to graduate schools or corporate training programs in which they have no interest anyway.

The world is absurd. Why would so many parents unthinkingly put their children through so much pressure and misery? So that one day the kids can be just as pressured and miserable as their parents?

Another consideration about schools, aside from academic pressure, is the problem of bullying. Schools are increasingly paying attention to the problem of bullying and trying to find ways to stamp it out. Unfortunately, bullying is as old as time and can be practiced so subtly that even the most well-meaning administrator or teacher cannot suss it out. This is yet another reason for asking why your kid needs to be unhappy at school in the first place.

Right now, we have four kids in four different schools (including one in high school, boarding out of state). We take seriously the idea of different strokes. We want our kids to be in the right place for them—not the place that's necessarily the most prestigious or the most convenient. Carpool is nuts for us, but it's worth it, because we're getting our kids what they need.

So to circle back to the original question of this chapter: Should you pay your kids to get A's? Absolutely! If you do a great job at work, don't you expect a bonus or a raise, or at least a warm handshake and smile from the boss? Incentivize your kids to do well. And don't focus on the bad grades they may get from time to time. Focus on what they're doing well, because whatever you (or they) pay attention to . . . grows.

They'll get through school. For me, sixth grade was the three toughest years of my life. But now look at me—writing books! Believe me, if I can make a living, your kids will, too.

Bring the Joneses Down
to Your Level

In *Isn't That Rich?*, which I mentioned earlier, a wealthy father says about his son, "I wish I had his childhood, and I wish he had mine."

Often, we want to do for our kids all the things that our parents weren't able to do for us when we were growing up. So we overcompensate like mad, or maybe there's the age-old competition with the Joneses next door, to ensure that your kid has the latest, greatest, and frequently most expensive shiny new toy.

It's a little over the top, *n'est-ce pas*?

As alcoholics and addicts, we tend to overdo this rush to materialism, perhaps because we live our whole lives with a sense of vainly trying to make up for lost time.

The best thing to do, by the way, about keeping up with the Joneses comes from the late Quentin Crisp, who advised, in the stage play *An Evening with Quentin Crisp:* "Don't try to keep up with the Joneses. Instead, drag the Joneses down to your level."

In Hebrew, the word *geshem* means "rain," and the word *goshmyot*, the plural form of "rain," means "material things." The implication is that just as with rain, a certain amount is necessary. Too much isn't a good thing. We live in a time of astonishing abundance and affluence. How can we tell if we've crossed the line from *geshem* to *goshmyot*, from enough to way too much?

Unfortunately, there's no blinking red light that says, "Warning! You are overindulging your children!" There is no bright line test. It's a feel thing. In this chapter, let's talk about money, stuff, and where to draw the line.*

I'm a walking, talking ATM. That's fine. I'm glad I have the skills to pay the bills. I was an indulged child.

As a recovering alcoholic, I struggle with my concept of finances, oscillating between a desire to live a rich, abundant life and at the same time not being certain that I deserve that kind of life, and not being certain how to create the money necessary to sustain it. I had to come to terms with my own attitude toward money, and try to find some clarity and even spirituality in the subject, if I was going to model a healthier relationship toward money than the one I had witnessed in my home growing up.

One of the things I learned in a sales training course is that when a couple comes to buy something expensive, like a car or furniture, or even when they simply are discussing how to handle their own finances, there are actually six voices at the table, not just two. His father and mother, her father and mother, him, and her—those are the six people who are debating whether and how to spend, save, or both. No wonder couples talk so much about money—it isn't a two-way argument, it's a six-way free-for-all.

Another formative experience I had with money came about the age of twelve. I was old enough to bicycle to the newsstand to buy a newspaper and some candy or whatever. I'd already developed a deep fascination with the printed word, which most certainly led to my career choice. One afternoon I bought

---

* We are often better at doing lines than drawing them—or drawing inside them.

two copies of the *New York Post,* the early edition and the late edition, because I wanted to see what the differences were.

I wanted to see what stories moved around from one edition to the next, what was added, what was cut, and so on. I was studying the two newspapers when my father came home from work and saw that I had bought two copies of the same day's newspaper. He went on a tirade. He yelled at me for being so crazy as to waste money on two newspapers when one would do.

I recall that I did not have the opportunity to explain to him the nature of my experiment and why I had actually bought the two copies of the newspaper. It was a bitter moment. I later learned that it was a formative one, giving me the sense that when it came to money, I was an idiot, not to be trusted with even small amounts.

I tell these stories not simply to play victim. Instead, my hope is that you will take a moment to consider the formative experiences that shaped your attitudes toward money, for better or worse. Did your parents tell you that money didn't grow on trees? Did you grow up with a sense that there wasn't enough? Was money used as a weapon or a tool for buying affection, as was the case in my home? What really went on behind that white picket fence of yours?

The book is called *Sober Dad,* but it might as well be called *Conscious Dad,* because I'm asking you to become conscious about pretty much every attitude you hold toward pretty much every aspect of life. Now, money. Whatever we don't recognize in ourselves, we pass on to our children. So now is a wonderful time to consider where you are with money—what it means to you, what power it has in your life, whether your associations, early and later, were positive or otherwise.

Money isn't love.

If it were, the richest people would automatically be the happiest, and we all know that's not so. Money solves the money problem, but it can create other problems as well. Every wealthy person, from Warren Buffett on down, grapples with the issue of "affluenza," the sickness that comes from having too much, too soon.

We all know the expression, from shirtsleeves to shirtsleeves in three generations, and if you don't know it, it means the first generation makes the money, the second generation spends the money, and the third generation is broke. Some families do better with money over the long haul than others. The Rockefellers are just as wealthy as they ever were. Ditto the Kennedys. The poor Vanderbilts, however, are by and large not exactly poor, but not exactly rich, either.

Money isn't love.

Money can provide us with ways of expressing love, because money allows us to be generous with loved ones, with causes that matter to us, with the homeless person asking for a handout.

Money allows us to live nicely, to have a home in a congenial part of town where our kids grow up seeing that if they work hard, they, too, can live well. It's a good message for kids to come home to.

At the same time, money can be a tool for controlling others. If you don't do as I say, I will cut you off financially. That's not generosity; that's sickness.

I know that you've already got a lot on your plate, but in addition to everything else you'll be doing with and for your children, you will also be shaping, consciously and unconsciously, subtly and overtly, how they feel about money, and how they feel about themselves. Unless you take the time to uncover any negative messages you may associate with money, chances are you'll pass along those same messages to your children.

What did I do to get from where I was to where I am now? I studied money. I read book after book about abundance. I learned that there's a difference between a mentality of abundance, in which we recognize that we live in a God-given, generous world where there is always enough, and usually a little bit more, or we have a poverty mentality, also known as coming from lack, which tells us that we don't have enough, there won't be enough, and it's only going to get worse.

I recognize now that in my younger years I ping-ponged between those two poles, abundance and lack. My father had been raised by parents who were quite wealthy as they went through the Depression—they lived on Fifth Avenue in Manhattan and had servants through the worst years of the worldwide economic crisis. But they went through the Depression nonetheless.

My paternal grandfather never bought my grandmother a new car. He never bought himself one, either. At eighty-two, he still rode the New York subway to work. They could've had a nice home in Florida and played golf all winter, but it was not for him. Money was something that you just didn't spend. You never knew.

My mother's family, by contrast, was extremely generous. Was it because I was the Columbus baby, the first child in the family born in the New World? Or were they just simply generous people to begin with? Probably a little bit of both. So it's not surprising that I would oscillate between an attitude of abundance and the gloomiest form of poverty thinking.

And what about you? What message are you modeling for your children about money?

The middle ground I seek as a parent is that sweet spot where

our kids lack for none of the necessities and some nice extras
. . . but not so much that they become spoiled or accustomed
to getting whatever they want whenever they want it.

We've taken some nice family vacations, and then there
have been other holiday periods where the money wasn't there,
so we stayed home. They have nice clothing but nothing with
a designer label showing. We have always tried to impress
upon them, through word and deed, that money is great, but
you don't need it at any given moment to have a great time. My
favorite nonfamily things are going to meetings, going to the
gym, running marathons, singing with my chorus, doing yoga,
and reading books.

My gym membership is typically my greatest luxury. I like
nice shoes, but I don't have a closetful. I get nervous when the
UPS truck laden with Amazon boxes stops too frequently at
our house. I think my kids see that I get much more pleasure
from my library card than from my MasterCard.

When we go to sporting events, we typically don't have
the best seats in the house. The price of sports tickets is crazy
today, and when you need six, you're more likely to see us in the
bleachers than in the box seats. On some level, I do wish that I
could have my kid sitting in the proverbial front row, where ball
players can smile at them and toss them balls. The good news
is that when you go to minor league games, you can practically
sit in the dugout for ten bucks. Ditto college sports—great seats,
cheap.

I would love to take my family to Europe in the summer to
sightsee, or to Switzerland in December to ski. I know plenty
of other families who do just that. I don't think it's the end of
the world that my kids aren't experiencing ultra-first-class or
flying private, or doing a lot of the things that truly wealthy
families do.

Instead, my kids know these things are available. I don't want to make it sound as though they have been through deprived childhoods. We've done some pretty cool things—Disney cruises, fly-fishing in Oregon, getaways to Florida in the dead of winter. But we do these things simply because they're fun, not because I'm trying to prove something to them or anyone else, control them, or compensate for shortcomings in my own childhood or psyche.

In a perfect world, they might do kitchen chores without so much grumbling. But they do them. I hope that my own confused nature toward money isn't as obvious to them as it is to me. I like nice things as much as the next person, and I'm thrilled when I can provide nice things to my wife and children.

I hope we have been successful—time will tell—at helping them understand the value of a dollar.

Speaking of chores, if you want to get your kids to do stuff, I find the advice in *How to Talk So Kids Will Listen & Listen So Kids Will Talk* by Adele Faber and Elaine Mazlish[18] to be very effective. It boils down to this: *use the fewest possible words.*

Kids think that the fewer words you use, the more serious you must be.

Compare and contrast:

"Tommy, do you think you could put down your Legion of Doom game on your iPhone for a minute and put some of the dishes in the dishwasher? Mommy and Daddy had a long day and it's so nice when we see our children stepping up and helping out around the house."

Your kid won't even look up from Legion of Doom.

You're doomed.

But every kid will understand this:

"Dishes. Dishwasher. Now."

What's the point? I believe in generosity, and I believe in

giving our kids the broadest possible range of experiences and fun. I also expect them to behave decently, do their homework, do their chores, and be good people. Money can't buy happiness, but it certainly can rent it. So go make some, save some, and spend the rest on your wife and kids.

MAN-UP MESSAGE 15

Leave Your Teens to
Their Own Devices

(But Only after Imparting
Some Rules and Common Sense)

Three teenagers (and an eight-year-old) currently live under the same roof with my wife and me; four teenagers, if you count me as one, too.

The stakes for everything are seemingly higher now. And yet, the teen years don't have to be nightmarish. I'm thinking that what little success we are having with ours has to do with the concept that I shared earlier, the expectation of the teenage years as a period of counter-dependence.

It's all about perspective.

If you look at your teenagers with shock and dismay and ask, "Who are these unruly people who ignore absolutely everything I say?" you're headed for trouble.

Few families have found that they could increase punishment until morale improved.

On the other hand, you can take the philosophical approach and say, "I love my kids. They are going through an age-appropriate phase in which several things are happening. First, they are taking their cues not from their parents but from the group, which means that I have far less sway than I once did. From a developmental standpoint, this is exactly where they are supposed to be. It may not be fun for me, but I can certainly get through it."

If you can take that attitude, life will not be a series of brutal battles pitting you and your spouse against your kids—or worse, a Hobbesian war of all against all. Moreover, teens are going through all kinds of hormonal and physical changes that are all too easy for me to forget, because once upon a time, I went through them, too. I'm reminded of the exchange from *West Side Story*:

> Officer Krupke: When I was your age—
> Troubled Kid: You was never my age.

Well, I was their age. I remember one time, on a family trip to Arizona, we were visiting a clothing store. I was fifteen. My father called me over to show me a leather jacket, and instead of acknowledging what a beautiful jacket it was—and it was indeed beautiful—I lashed out at him for no reason. Who did he think he was to call me over that way? What was I, a dog? Or words to that effect.

We both stood there stunned by my outburst, which was as inappropriate as it was ill timed.

I certainly didn't get that leather jacket.

I just remember being so puzzled. Where did that explosiveness come from in me? I had never seen it before.

I can't tell you about the specific hormones that are released by the process of puberty or whatever is going on in the teenager's body and mind. All I know is that I went through it, too. So I recognize that for whatever reason known only to the mind of God, teens have really big emotions, and they often cannot control their outbursts.

Now, I won't tolerate certain language, as I've expressed elsewhere in the book. There are certain words that, if used on me or another family member, will merit some type of consequence. With my kids growing up, that now usually consists of spending some quality time thinking in their bedroom or the loss of some privilege, typically electronic in nature. But by and large, I just try to let them be as big and loud as they need to be. If they could control it, they probably would. And in any event, I really have to ask myself—do I want to be a father or a cop? Am I going to call them on every single outburst or incident? Or am I going to let the small things ride and instead pick my battles?

Taking on this approach requires me to confront my perfectionist streak—my expectation of perfection from myself (if I were a perfect parent, they wouldn't be doing this) and my expectation of perfection in others (they better get their acts together or else). In reality, one day I hope to get my act together, too. But by the time I do, that will probably be my *last* act.

Now let's talk about *you* for a moment. Work/life balance is awfully hard to maintain in a time when you carry your entire work life on your smartphone. Can you manage not to email, text, or make calls in the evening? Your partner wants you present in the house and not staring at your device. It's also a question of what you're modeling for your kids. Perhaps, as the parent of a teenager, you've recently noticed that your teen doesn't seem to be able to exist without that smartphone you got him or her firmly planted in hand at all hours of the day. Have you found yourself complaining, "My kid is always staring at the phone, so we never talk anymore!"? Reality check: Is your phone always in your hand, too? Remember that sense of personal responsibility. Is "family time" a big lie, and just a chance to check Facebook? Put the device down and look your loved ones in the eye. It may be the only eye contact they receive all day.

In any event, when you're home, be home. Be present. It's the best "present" you could give your family.

Think of different ways to work with the forms of media that bombard us and our kids throughout the day (rather than just working against it, or banning it from your home, which can lead to other issues). For example, I count the time my kids spend on their phone making things differently than I do the time they just spend mindlessly browsing stuff or playing games. In other words, I differentiate making videos from simply viewing them, because this forces kids to be creative, to perform entertainingly, and to do whatever is necessary (within legal and moral limits) to attract a following on YouTube. So if my kids are making videos, I see that as an act of creativity, something to be encouraged, instead of simply more time wasted watching other people.

I actually went to the store with my boys this past weekend and bought them a camera, a screen, and a first-rate microphone so that they (and I) could make better-quality YouTube videos for our various audiences. The reality is that technology is where kids live today, so if it's possible to encourage your kids to create instead of to consume, it's not the end of the world.

I've seen various books that claim that there are mental benefits to playing video games. This may well be, but every time I pass one of those gaming rooms for young adults, I see losers who smoke. So, as Linus once told Lucy in a *Peanuts* cartoon, tell your statistics to shut up.

The next challenge is determining what your kids will watch on TV. This evolves a bit from young child to teen. We do not have cable, satellite, or even rabbit ears. As a result, while our kids do have access to YouTube, Hulu, and Netflix, more popular culture content than you can shake a stick at, they don't watch over-the-air TV.

We did this for a reason—to spare them the inappropriate sorts of shows that even the traditional networks carry, and also, perhaps equally important, to spare them the thousands and thousands of commercials that they would be watching in any given year. What's wrong with commercials? Aside from stoking a never-ending fire of materialism in your children and in yourself, commercials give children an entirely inaccurate vision of life.

As the late, great motivational speaker and author Zig Ziglar said, commercials give kids (and adults) the idea that practically any life problem can be solved in thirty seconds, if you will just buy something. Not exposing kids to those thousands of hours of commercials has been one of the smartest moves we've ever made.

A couple from my AA home group babysat our kids about six years ago, when they were between five and seven years old. When we came home, they told us, "You guys are the greatest parents in the world!"

We didn't exactly feel that way, but we were up for a compliment.

"Your kids have never heard of Ronald McDonald!"

They had not. Our kids have never been through a drive-thru. Not only does this make for better-quality eating, but my wife cooks a full meal (often two, because I'm a stubborn vegetarian) pretty much every single night. We are extremely health conscious and don't want to expose ourselves or our kids to chemicals, additives, preservatives, and high levels of sugar, salt, and fat, which can be found in pretty much every aspect of corporate food today.

We are not insane—you could put us in any half-decent restaurant and we will easily and happily find choices on the menu. We're not micro or macro or Paleo or anything else. We just try to eat right, and I am every bit as much a compulsive overeater as I am an alcoholic—probably more so. But there's something to be said for family meals with real food and all electronics off.

As you can tell from this book, I don't have too many strict rules for my kids once you get past the basic "don't bug each other or us" dictum. But one rule is inviolate: No technology at meals. We don't have laptops open (except for me doing my email at breakfast before work—I know. Do as I say, not as I do).

The kids may not have phones out during meals. There is no TV or other form of screen on. When we go to restaurants, the kids have never been allowed to use a device like a phone or an iPad while they are waiting for the food to arrive or while they're eating. I feel so sad when I see entire families at a restaurant table, each one pecking away at a device, no one looking at or listening to any of the other family members.

I'm not suggesting that our dinner conversations are as scintillating as President Jefferson's. I am saying that we sit and listen to each other in an atmosphere of peace and quiet. It's great. I understand that fewer and fewer families do put on these kinds of meals, so my wife gets full credit for making the effort, night after night. Her challenge is compounded by the fact that, as I mentioned, three of our children are teenagers, and two of them are less likely to say thanks or pay a compliment for even a great meal. But my wife does it anyway—way to go, baby! Love you so much!

I've consulted on creativity to two television networks—NBC and The WB. At one point, NBC flew me to San Francisco to speak at a convention of employees of their owned and operated local television stations across the country. Fascinated, I sat in on some of the other sessions. One speaker said words that sent chills down my spine. "Our job," he told his audience of fellow local television executives, "is to make the family look up from the dinner table."

It's hard to have meaningful conversations, or even coherent thoughts, if a shiny, colorful device is literally trying to get and hold your attention. There's no case to be made for screens at mealtime, unless of course it's business owner dad on his laptop, checking emails, as he eats breakfast.

Okay, I just busted myself.

Do I let my kids "sneak" some extra techno? Yes, I do. As long as it's within limits—nothing violent, nothing obscene, and no games that look like they will turn my kids' brains to putty. Some of these games are so habit forming and, dare I say, addictive that I voice my displeasure quickly and firmly. Do they listen when I'm not around? Who knows?

The last piece about technology that you want to impress on your kids is the danger of posting online. Most kids have been warned about adults masquerading as children, trolling for children as sexual partners online. If you start that lecture and your kid rolls his or her eyes, you can probably consider that base covered. The one thing that younger people just don't realize is how damaging their social media footprint can be later on. If you have a teen in your house, remember what I said about the years of counter-dependence. The issue nowadays is that as teens try to "spread their wings," they can be making some decisions that will stay with them for life. For all to see.

I understand that you can take a sexually revealing photo of a person or a couple and post it on Snapchat, secure in the knowledge that it will vanish within eight seconds. But what's to stop one of the recipients from whipping out a second smartphone and taking a photo of the image on Snapchat, and then posting that? It happens every day of the year. Teens don't think of that. The amount of DIY porn online is staggering (so I'm told!). Kids don't realize that the Internet is the first thing that actually ignores the law of gravity. What goes up *never* comes down. Schools are looking at social media platforms to see whom to admit and, quite frankly, whom to expel. Employers certainly scan social media for clues as to the proclivities of new hires. And I think more and more, parents themselves are looking up other kids to see if they are suitable playmates for their sons and daughters.

The damage that a person can do to a reputation—damage that can last a lifetime—can happen in just a few seconds. The stakes are so much higher than they ever were. I thank God that there was no such thing as social media back when I was a teenager or in my early twenties and still drinking. I can only imagine what sort of stuff I would have photographed and posted back then. In my mind, it would've been funny. When I went to look for a college admission or a job, it might have been less funny, after all.

It's your job to help your teen navigate these choppy waters and come out on the other side. Perhaps with some bumps and bruises, but again, with the chance to hit the ground running rather than just hitting the ground.

So there you have it. Coping with technology, by one who was there. It's not about whether your kid is a good kid or a bad kid. Bad kids steal trucks. Good kids destroy their own brains through overuse of technology and their reputations through inappropriate posts, whether verbal or visual. What can you do? Just talk to your kids. Or as Ronald Reagan said, trust but verify. And set limits, and pray.

Now that we've got a concept of what we don't want to be (enmeshed emotionally with our children), let's focus now on what we do want to be—healthy sources of love and attention for our children. Remember that your teenager is not looking for a best friend. If you are, run, don't walk, to your sponsor's home or your therapist's office and explain that your greatest desire in life is to be your child's best friend.

See how well that goes over, and see if they can coach you out of that mentality. A child needs a parent. A teenager, though learning to spread those wings, still needs a parent— even in the throes of counter-dependence. It's the child's job to test boundaries, and it's your job to lovingly resist when they do so. (When my oldest daughter was five, I said, "Are you testing my limits?" To which she replied, charmingly, "Yes, Daddy. I am testing your *lemons*.")

When my children were little, I had a theory that they wanted to lose every argument with me. They wanted to argue to test their own power, but at the same time, they wanted the security of knowing that their father and their mother provided healthy limits. Bedtime was bedtime. Okay, you could squeeze five more minutes out of us, but you couldn't stay up until midnight, order in pizza, and watch YouTube videos. You're six years old, for God's sake! Go to bed!

Even if Mommy is out of the house for the evening, you still can't have ice cream for dinner. You have to brush and floss. You're not allowed to hit your brother or sister, and you're not allowed to use certain language that you heard outside the home. The father's job, as I've said, is not to be a prison warden. But it is also not your job to be their best friend. A friend, at times (although you and your partner are the only ones who can discipline them). But not their *best* friend. Let them go out and make their own friends. Your job is to be the loving person who is present and attentive. All of this remains the same with a teenager, even as the dynamics in your relationship with your growing child seem to change overnight.

It often happens in families that the mothers are in charge of the core stuff—stocking the refrigerator, making sure that there are socks in the drawer. Somehow, for all the talk about changing gender roles, the grunt work still often falls on Mom. To the extent that you can assist her with that, you would be wise. There's no reason for a man to leave a dirty dish in the sink.

So take your kids out to buy new shoes, or make sure their toothbrushes are newish, and so on, do those things. Everyone will be happier.

But at the same time, the special role of the father in a home, as our pediatrician once explained to us, is "minister of fun." When the children are little, it's up to you to figure out fun excursions for the family. The zoo? Rock climbing? Minor league baseball? Definitely. Chuck E. Cheese's? Pass. Talk to other dads. Go online. Buy books about fun things to do for kids in your region. But definitely be the minister of fun. If you don't do it, it's too much to ask your partner to do. She's busy enough. So while you are not expected to be the best friend of your children, you are expected to show up and play with them when they are little, and in your role as "minister of fun," plan excursions.

As your children get older, you will want to take a step back from the planner of fun and instead let them create their own fun. Let them call their friends and make plans when they come of age. You don't have to be the camp counselor forever. I'm happy to fund the occasional movie for my kids, and yes, I will take them to the drugstore to buy the occasional unhealthy snack (why is it that you go to the drugstore for unhealthy snacks?).

By the time your kids are adolescents, you can dial back on the ministry of fun thing and let them create their own happiness. By the time they get to be teenagers, all you can do is hope that the parenting you did from age zero to twelve will stick with them and help them navigate the many risks that kids face today, online and off. If you can get a straight answer out of your fifteen-year-old when you ask, "Where did you go and who were you with?" then you belong in the Parents Hall of Fame.

If you've got healthy boundaries with your kids, by the time they reach their teenage years, they'll call on you if they need you, which is as it should be. I remember my dad had a terribly difficult time when my sisters became teens. Somehow, they had absorbed the idea in earlier years that their responsibility was to butter up Dad. He would come home from work and complain, "I feel fat." Automatically, they would respond, "You look great!" And so on. (I'm so glad I'm publishing this under a pseudonym.)

When my sisters got a little older, around thirteen or fourteen, neither they nor I felt the responsibility to assuage his feelings. I took things a little too far, in my own adorable way. When my father said, "I feel fat," I would respond, "You *look* fat."

In some ways, my father never made the pivot from expecting his daughters to be his cheerleaders to acknowledging that they were young adults in their own right. I remember once a cousin of ours had taken a picture of one of my sisters in front of a hotel. It was a hot summer day, and she was wearing shorts and a T-shirt.

My father looked at the photo and said, "She looks like a prostitute."

How do you even think something like that?

Ask Jack.

Daniel's, that is.

The message here is that as your children get bigger, they are going to need less of you, and you are going to get less of them. And that's as it should be. Let them grow, and let them go. If you insist on them staying stuck in an early childhood way of relating to you, you are not doing them a favor. Remember what my sponsor told me? "You may not have had a happy childhood, but you sure are having a long one." Don't let that happen to your kids.

Psychologists say that one of the greatest tragedies in life is either staying stuck in a particular phase of one's emotional development or trying to skip a phase before it's time. Alcoholic teens are in a great hurry to grow up. I certainly was. I wanted freedom from my crazy home. Instead, by practicing certain adult behaviors related to alcohol and girls, I caused huge problems for myself and those around me.

If you let your children be, if you just let them develop, if you don't force them to advance, and if you don't force them to stay put, but instead embrace each change in their lives with a private sense of excitement and delight, you'll be doing them a great favor.

My wonderful grandmother used to say, "Every season is beautiful." So it is with your children. Take lots of photos and keep the Magic Moments file current, but don't live in the past and don't force them to live in the past. Again, let them be. This is the ultimate demonstration of healthy boundaries.

I once heard a speaker in an Al-Anon meeting say that she was good with the "let live" part of "live and let live," but she had a much harder time with the "live" option. I'm not suggesting she was dead. I am saying that she found it difficult to make a life for herself, having been so tied to the mood swings of her alcoholic husband.

So the message in this section of the chapter is "get a life." This is unbelievably important when your children are little, but if you don't have this worked out by the time they are teens . . . well, hop to it. The Al-Anon Do's and Don'ts, available at any Al-Anon meeting or online, is up there with my two other favorite pieces of Twelve Step literature, both found in the Big Book: "The Doctor's Opinion" and the last two pages of "The Keys of the Kingdom." (Check all of them out if you're not familiar with them.) The Do's and Don'ts remind us to "find recreation and hobbies." This is absolutely great advice for parents. It is essential that you have activities that are uniquely yours or something you share with your partner, something of which your children are not a part. I run marathons. I sing with choruses. I chant the Torah in my synagogue services, which requires a lot of time and preparation.

My kids are welcome to come to my races or concerts or presentations, but these are *my* things. It's important to have things that are uniquely yours and that you do *not* share with your children. John Bradshaw, one of the great experts on families, healthy and otherwise, says that one of the biggest burdens a child can bear is the unlived life of his parents. The concept of "live and let live" applies to your children, but to be more precise, the "let live" applies to them and the "live" applies to you. Don't be like that woman in the Al-Anon meeting. Find things that bring you joy. Do them. Live your own life.

Take your wife out on date nights. Take her on the occasional overnight trip, if you can find appropriate help to watch your kids. Don't give kids the specifics. Go out and live your life, and let them understand that there are certain things that adults keep private. Not all of your business is their business.

My wife will chortle, because all too often I tell my kids way too much about what's going on in my brain. I talk with them a lot about what I do and where I go. I'm trying to model for them the idea that life is about going for it, finding exciting things to do, doing them, and learning from those experiences. I want them to have a "go for it" mentality themselves, so I'm trying to model it.

The main point here is that you get to go out there and do fun things, and you don't have to tell your kids all about it. One of the greatest gifts you as a parent can give your children is *living your own life*. Modeling this approach is important for kids at all ages, but know that this approach is especially influential for teens, who are in the midst of trying to figure out how to live theirs.

This doesn't mean that when you have small children, it's time to become a scratch golfer. I love to play golf, even though I'm terrible at it, but I instinctively knew that slinging my sticks over my shoulder when our children were infants and giving a happy wave to my wife on a Sunday morning was a terrible idea. Golf just takes too much time.

Bowling, on the other hand, does not. Neither does a chorus rehearsal. Neither does a yoga class. You can certainly find an hour to an hour and a half a day to get some exercise in, a walk, coffee with a friend, or something nourishing for your body and soul. If you don't take care of you, who will? In Al-Anon, they love to discuss the metaphor of the flight attendant who says that in the event of an emergency, put your own oxygen mask on first. Where are you getting oxygen from?

I once saw a speaker who concluded by holding a cup and saucer in one hand and a pitcher full of water in the other. She explained that you have to keep yourself filled up before you can do anything for anyone else. So she filled the cup halfway and asked the audience, "Is it okay to start doing things for other people now that your cup is half filled?" A few people in the audience said yes, and she shook her head.

She then filled up the cup and asked the audience, "Now is

it okay to start sharing with other people, since your own cup is filled up?" The audience shouted out their approval.

Wrong, the speaker told us. Then, to our shock and amazement, she poured the entire contents of the pitcher into the cup, which overflowed onto the saucer and then onto the floor. This violated all of our notions about keeping things tidy, and we were howling with laughter and shock.

"*This* is when you can give to others," the speaker calmly explained, as the water cascaded over the top of the cup and the saucer onto the stage. "You can only share with other people when your own cup is overflowing."

So that's your job. Keep your own cup overflowing, in every way—emotionally, physically, spiritually. Recognize that if you come from an alcoholic home, or from any kind of unhealthy home (let's not use the words *dysfunctional* or *toxic*), you may have a tendency to practice enmeshment instead of healthy boundaries and detachment.

Do what you need to do to resolve those issues if you recognize them in yourself, either in a therapist's office or in the Al-Anon fellowship or, ideally, in both places. You don't have to be your child's best friend. That's not what they want. They want you to be their dad. **Their *sober* dad.** So be that.

Your Kids Don't Need to Know *Everything* about You

Last night, after dinner, I was sitting around with my oldest daughter and my wife, eying a plate of chocolate chip cookies they had baked. I can't have any chocolate chip cookies, because if I have one, I have to have a thousand. As the line goes, I can handle the two thousand calories a day. It's the eight thousand calories at night that are killing me.

But while we were chatting and I was gazing at the cookies, a memory from my teenage years suddenly returned. I had been at the home of a friend who offered me a plate of freshly baked chocolate chip cookies. Back then, I had neither a program nor any reason to say no, so I dug in. I ate a couple of the cookies, and then I ate a few more. My friend was looking at me as if I was a little crazy, but when you're sixteen years old and an incipient food addict, what could be better than a plate of freshly baked chocolate chip cookies?

It wasn't until I had polished off the entire plate that he looked at me guiltily and admitted, "We laced those cookies with marijuana."

I didn't get high. The 1970s-grade grass, however much had been baked in, didn't leave me baked in the least. Nonetheless, with one exception, that was the last time I ever spoke to that person, from that day to this.

He could've told me after one cookie, of course.

Or even before the first cookie.

I mention all this because, for whatever reason, I felt impelled to tell my wife and daughter about that moment. They were suitably appalled on my behalf, but for whatever reason, I couldn't stop. I was the same way with the truth as I had been with chocolate chips.

"I actually used marijuana twice," I admitted, not having been asked.

My daughter, straight-laced to the max, spun toward me.

"Daddy!" she said plaintively. "You're kidding, aren't you?"

"I didn't inhale," I explained lamely, deeply regretting the admission.

I then went on to explain that you really only get high when you inhaled the smoke and kept it in your lungs. I remembered dimly that Bill Clinton had made the same claim—that he had tried it twice but inhaled neither time—and no one believed him, either.

To make matters worse, my wife chimed in, "I actually got high. In the woods, with friends."

My daughter looked shocked. Not just shocked—betrayed.

"How could you?" she asked, suddenly realizing that her parents weren't fabulous; they were idiots.

"It was the seventies," I said on my own behalf, as if that explained everything.*

But not to her.

I felt so terrible. I hadn't lied to my daughter, but I had offered her a bit of truth that she really could have done without. So in this chapter, I'd like to delve into the overall question

---

* Of course, if you were around in the 1970s, that *did* explain everything.

of how much of your past life you need to share with your child, or with your partner, for that matter.

In other words, does rigorous honesty mean you have to say everything?

About fifteen years ago, Pamela Anderson became notorious for a sex tape that she and her musician husband had made. Somehow it had been leaked and went viral on the Internet. This was well before the explosion of DIY porn, and people wanted an explanation. What exactly was she going to tell her children?

"We're going to tell them that back then, Mommy and Daddy filmed everything," she explained, as if an incredibly stupid explanation might somehow satisfy her children.

I don't know if she stuck to that story, or if the matter ever came up with her kids. All I know is that sometimes the truth of our past lives is simply too much to ask our children to bear.

Joe and Charlie, the speakers who put on The Big Book Comes Alive seminars, point out that alcoholics get to lead two lives—the insane, alcoholic one, and then the sober one. Is it really necessary to go into great detail with our kids about that prior life?

Every couple has to set their own rules, but the suggestion I would offer is that it's just not a great idea. My kids know, of course, that I'm sober. They've been to meetings with me, and they've given me medallions on my birthdays over the years. But they've never heard me share openly from the podium about my prior life, nor, most likely, will they ever. They know that there is a long family history of alcoholism on my side of the family, and that if they get involved with alcohol or drugs, they could pay a price. I'm fine with them knowing that. They don't need to know about the specifics—the blackouts, the inappropriate encounters, the firings, and the rest of the steps on my path toward my bottom.

My wife and I made a pact while we were still dating, and once it became clear that we were serious, that we would not share details with each other about past relationships. I'm glad we made that decision. Again, this is a decision that every couple has to make for themselves, but at least for us, we made the right choice. There's a wonderful old Carly Simon song called "No Secrets" about a couple who knows all the facts, all the past lovers, everything. And then she sings, "Sometimes I wish that I never, ever knew some of those secrets of yours."

The girl I dated prior to meeting my wife actually had a picture of herself and her ex-boyfriend up on the wall of her Manhattan apartment. This bothered me, and I asked her if she would consider taking it down. She chose not to, which gives you some sense of how that relationship went. I don't keep photos of exes. To my knowledge, neither does my wife, although I certainly have never rummaged through her stuff (and never will). There's a strong case to be made for letting the past remain in the past, and not overburdening one's partner with information, photos, and memories that testify to intimacies with others.

You and your partner can do whatever you want, but that's what's worked for us.

To come back to the kids, they are not here to hear my Fifth Step. I did that already with sponsors and occasionally friends in AA when I went in for the "annual housecleanings" that the Big Book mentions. As my kids get older, I do not intend to tell them about my misadventures. Those events may seem laughable now, but my children see me as I am today. I don't really understand the point of diminishing myself in their eyes in the name of commitment to rigorous, if misguided, honesty.

I don't lie to my children. They understand, to varying degrees, that I was not always an upstanding citizen in my drinking days. They've never asked for specifics, and I would never share specifics, even if asked. Why I had to mention the puffs on two joints, I don't know. All it would do is encourage them to make the same stupid mistakes I made. If you feel differently, do it differently. I'm just telling you what has worked for me. I've always tried to be as honest as possible, however, with my children, whenever honesty would not hurt them. I'll give you some examples.

The day before my twin sons' fourth birthday, one of them was nearly killed in a freak accident; he was playing with some other children who somehow pushed a heavy podium that landed, hard, on his chest, severing an artery. He nearly bled out on the operating table and remained hospitalized for a week after the lifesaving operation. The emergency surgeon keeps a photo of my son on his desk to this day, which tells me all I need to know about how close we came to a bad ending.

At the time of the accident, my oldest was six, and as I said, the boys were four. I remember night after night patiently answering their questions before bedtime about the nature of the accident, why it happened, what the treatment course involved, why he had staples in his chest after the surgery, when the scar would go away, and so on and so forth.

It just seemed like the right thing to do to answer their questions as openly and as fully as I could. I thought that perhaps if they sensed I was hiding something, they would think things were even worse than they had been, and they had been bad enough. I don't regret being straightforward with them.

Almost a decade has passed since that terrifying event, and the subject doesn't come up much anymore. I'd like to think that the straight answers I gave them helped to remove some of the trauma from the situation. Although who knows?

On occasion, my boys have wondered if I had girlfriends

prior to my wife. It's a question I ignore. It's just not an answer they need.

The subject of sex has really never arisen for our kids. Somehow, they all figured things out on their own. I remember when my boys were around nine years old, they came home giggling like crazy because obviously someone at school had set them straight on the facts of life. A bit earlier than I might have hoped, but what are you going to do? When they asked me if their understanding was correct, I told them, "Yes, but this is simply not a subject for this age, so we can talk about it again in a few years."

I didn't want to give them the sense that sex was wrong or bad. I did want them to understand that they had glommed onto things a lot earlier than I might have hoped for, and that the conversation was over, respectfully but firmly, for some time to come.

My wife and I are raising our kids in a religious community whose culture does not permit dating until one is ready for marriage, typically in one's early twenties. It blows my mind that my teenage children are only slightly younger than I was when I became sexually active.* What was I thinking? Obviously, I wasn't. But does it really make sense for people too young to drive legally to play with fire?

If my kids ask me about my own experiences, they won't learn much. All they really need to know is how my wife and I feel about what is permissible and what is not for them right now. They will make their own choices, and in today's crazy world, I hope they don't feel pressured into making short-term decisions that potentially could have long-term consequences. I went through some pretty horrible experiences as a result of

---

* I sure hope they never read this book.

my premature excursions into physical intimacy, and I do not wish that same pain on my children, or anyone's children.

Let's move away from sex to the topic of money. My kids are intensely interested in how much money I make and how much money we have. It's just natural, I suppose. They want to know if we are millionaires. Once again, it's none of their business! I don't believe that children should have access to their parents' bank statements. It's just none of their business. When I was growing up, the only indication I had that my parents were doing well would be a vacation we took or a new car in the driveway. Otherwise, I had no idea, and I didn't need to know. So that much I don't share with my kids.

On the other hand, I do want them to know how the world really works—that many of the most successful people in our society are individuals who start their own businesses. I am a business owner, and my kids know a great deal about my business. They know who some of my clients are, they know who is on my team, they know who quit or got fired, and they know why.

I tell them perhaps more than the average parent because I want them to understand that life isn't just about building a résumé and getting a job. It's about following your dream and then finding ways to turn that dream into a livelihood, if you so choose. I was deeply influenced by a book I read as a teen about New York politics. A mayor of New York City had been the son of a U.S. senator from New York. The book recounted the story of how labor leaders had come to his father's Senate office and made a secret pledge. When the son became mayor decades later, he reminded those same union leaders of the pledge they had made in his father's Senate office. The union leaders were incredulous. How could the mayor possibly have known about that?

"I was playing under the desk," the mayor replied.

That story stayed with me because it made me realize that some kids grow up with a very clear sense of how the world works. I didn't have that in the least. My father would speak about his work, but in general terms. I seldom met adults who would talk openly about the real world. I have wanted my kids from the start to be exposed to the broadest possible range of adults.

I bring home clients who are world famous and I bring home homeless people whom I've met in an AA meeting, and everything in between. I've had an intention throughout my children's childhoods to expose them, in appropriate ways, of course, to as much of the adult world as I possibly could.

I talk about business situations with them, because I want them to know that running a business isn't easy, and that if you work hard, you can overcome problems and succeed. So many of the most successful people in history, from Andrew Carnegie and John D. Rockefeller in the nineteenth century to Bill Gates and Steve Jobs in modern times, had no higher education or didn't finish college.

Today, we allow young people to keep their fingers on the pause button of life for years and years. They may not even enter the workforce until their mid- to late twenties, depending on how much graduate education they receive. Is this an advantage? I'm not sure. Whatever my kids do, I want their real-world education to have begun while they were still adolescents. I want them to know how the world works.

My oldest daughter homeschooled in my office for one semester during eighth grade. She would listen in on negotiations with prospects, hear calls from unhappy clients, phone meetings with business colleagues, and everything else that went on over the course of my day. I think that was every bit as important an aspect of our homeschooling as anything we did in math or grammar.

When I got sober, I had already destroyed any chance of finding continued employment in the field for which I'd trained. I honestly have no idea how I survived financially for the first two years of my sobriety. I remember I house sat for a friend for one of those years, and I basically lived off credit card advances in the second year. I entered Debtors Anonymous the night before my second AA birthday and met a man who showed me how to start a business.

My kids can point out the donut shop where he sat me down, took out a single sheet of paper, and showed me how to start the business I've now run for twenty-two years. My kids know a lot about the rhythms of entrepreneurship, without knowing the specifics of how much I earn or how much I pay people. I think this is great.

My kids have seldom inquired as to the nature of our marriage. That's another area in which I will not provide information. I mentioned earlier how dangerous it is for a child to be triangulated into a marriage, to be used as a confidant by one or, worse, both parties in an unhappy relationship. I will not say that marriage has been easy, although we are approaching our seventeenth anniversary, which is a pretty good run in today's world.

My wife and I try very hard not to air our disputes or dirty laundry in front of our children. It's hard not to, because in the heat of the moment, things get said. All I can do is hope that our children recognize that despite occasional disagreements, my wife and I do love each other and are committed to our marriage and our home.

A common theme in most, if not all, parenting books is that the most important thing parents can provide their children is unity. Children, even small children, are unbelievably expert at exploiting differences between parents. They do so with the skill of arbitrageurs picking off tiny discrepancies between the Euro and the yen. It's not just about getting the extra half hour before bedtime or another bowl of ice cream. It's about seeing how much power the children can have vis-à-vis the parents.

My wife and I have not seen eye to eye on a number of important issues over the years, which is not surprising, given the fact that our backgrounds are radically different. I don't want to go into more detail because I don't want to expose my wife's anonymity, let alone my own. I will say that the most painful moments in the marriage have come when either of us felt undermined, especially in the eyes of a carefully observing child. To the extent that you can work out your differences over parenting policy, small and large, out of earshot of your children, I would urge you to do so.

One of the most important things a couple can do is recognize that marriage is complicated and that raising children is hard. There is no manual—alas, not even this book! Children do not come with their own instructions, and as they grow, they change. One size doesn't fit all. One size doesn't even fit for long. If golfers have swing coaches, and basketball players have coaches just to show them how to hit foul shots, doesn't it stand to reason that marriage and child rearing are too complex, and too important, to be do-it-yourself kinds of endeavors? Get outside help. There is so much wisdom to be had from competent therapists that it is almost criminal not to take advantage.

You've got to find someone good, and you've got to find someone who doesn't favor one parent over the other. Having a sounding board—someone to listen to our ideas and offer a broader perspective than the ones we bring from our own families and own expectations—has been invaluable over the course of the marriage. It just helps to have someone older and wiser whom I can call or even text and say, "This is what's going on. What do I do now?"

Our children are not aware, to my knowledge, that either my wife or I seek outside help. Again, this falls into the category of "none of their business." It's not something I would seek to hide from them. If they asked, I would answer frankly that I do get help. But it's just not germane to the parent-child conversation, so I don't bring it up.

The operating principle throughout the material I've shared in this chapter so far has to do with the division between privacy and secrecy. Secrecy is unhealthy; we are only as sick as our secrets. But privacy is fine. There are things I don't know about my wife, and there are things she doesn't know about me, not just in terms of our pasts, but also in terms of our present-day lives. And that's fine. We don't really need to know every single detail.

Similarly, I try to extend the courtesy of privacy to my children. I do not snoop in their rooms. I try never to enter their rooms without their permission, as a matter of fact, unless I have an awfully good reason for going in. I try to respect the fact that their room is their sanctuary and the only source of privacy they really have.

When they go to school, religious services, restaurants, or pretty much anywhere else, others are conscious of their behavior, and they have to conform to expectations. That's not just us; that's life. But in our home, I consider them worthy of enough trust and respect not to invade their personal spaces. I don't go in their closets. I don't go in their drawers. I'm not searching for contraband. Maybe I'm naïve, but I want to afford them the same sense of respect for their belongings that I hope they have for mine.

One of my biggest faults is that I have a big mouth. I like to be funny. I can do a phenomenal imitation of one of my brothers-in-law. It makes my sons laugh uncontrollably. My wife just rolls her eyes because she knows I'm setting a terrible example for them. But I just cannot help myself. I love to make them laugh. Bad Sober Daddy. So bad.

One of the things we learned in a parenting class early on is that most environments outside the home require very high levels of behavior. A kid cannot act out in school, or in a religious institution, with impunity. There are consequences for bad behavior. So kids naturally save most of their bad behavior for the home. Guess what? So do I!

I have to behave at work. I have to set an example for the team I lead, for the people in my workplace, and for my clients. So like my kids, I am most prone to act out when I'm home. Also, the bulk of the time I spend with my kids is in the evening, after a long day, so they're not necessarily getting me at my most buttoned up. It's a never-ending struggle for me to keep my mouth shut, to remain appropriate, and, in short, to be the kind of person who ought to be writing a book about being a sober dad. I would just rather make them laugh.

Am I always appropriate? No. I love to tell my sons inappropriate jokes. Nothing really awful, but silly stuff. I love to see their eyes widen and hear them howl with laughter. It's one of the most fun things there is. Do I cross the line in terms of appropriateness? Sometimes I do.

I don't know whether it's a copout or whether I'm sincere when I say that I'm just as good a father when I'm crossing lines and saying things I shouldn't be saying, and even doing that dead-on interpretation of my brother-in-law. It just shows my kids that I'm not perfect, and they don't have to be perfect, either.

To sum up, there's a lot about me that my children, and even my wife, need never know, and will never know. I try hard to remain appropriate in terms of subject matter and level of detail. They don't need to know everything about my past. I try to respect their privacy as well. And if I feel safe in my own home to cut loose and maybe cross the line, it's not the end of the world. I know just how much truth to tell my kids. Probably a little too much, but nothing that truly crosses the line.

I know where the real lines are, and for the most part, I work very hard at not crossing them. And I'm certain my kids are happier for it.

And Finally . . . an Ode to Joy

So far, this book may have given the impression that fatherhood is a series of problems to be solved, as opposed to a source of joy. If so, I would be selling short the whole experience. New dads have a lot of concerns going into fatherhood: Will I measure up? Will I be good enough as a parent? Will my kid be okay? What's going to happen? There are no real answers to these questions other than the experience will grow you and stretch you, if you allow it to, and you'll find inner resources that you didn't know you had.

Children themselves—other people's children, I mean—are not always the best advocates of becoming a parent. Pre-dads see them in supermarkets, sullen little beings commanding their parents to buy junk food or risk meltdowns. Before your own kids arrive, it's easy to focus in on the babies crying, the exhausted parents texting while their kids scream their heads off, and other manifestations of parenting-related misery. Newspaper stories about kids who do really bad things, or parents who do really bad things to kids, make people ask, who needs the aggravation?

Recently, I read a book that consisted of essays by people who have individually chosen not to have children. These are not people who biologically could not have children—they've simply decided they didn't want to be parents. So they all wrote essays and somebody put the essays together and published them in a book.

For all the craziness my wife and I have been through over the past seventeen years, I read the book with a measure of sadness for the authors of the essays. In many ways, they have no idea what life is about. The reasons they gave for not having children were pretty much what you would expect: They didn't have happy childhoods, or their careers came first, or they liked to travel. That sort of thing. Nobody's going to look back after you died and say, wow, he went to forty-seven countries. Or gosh, she might not have had kids, but she sure was a great mid-level executive at a tractor company. Or, what a collection of beer mugs he left behind!

As I've said, the role of human beings is to become an ancestor, and it's awfully hard to do that if you don't go through the strain and brain damage of becoming a parent. But there's so much more to it.

I treasure the time I spend with my children, one on one, in groups, or as an entire family. Our walls are covered with photo collections of the most magical moments we've shared together.

> The Disney cruise to Alaska, when I sprang for the extra $2,000—yes, I know that's a *lot* of money—to take my big three on a helicopter to a glacier, where they got to mush and play with actual Alaskan sled dogs.

> Taking my sons fly-fishing in Bend, Oregon.

> Dancing with my youngest daughter onstage at her ballet recital when she was about seven, in the father-daughter number.

> Helping our oldest find the right school for her junior and senior years of high school, and marveling at the courage she has displayed, boarding with a family 180 miles from our home, so that she can attend that school.

Reading to my children at bedtime.

Providing answers as best I could after my little boy's accident, which I described earlier.

Attending Yankees-Red Sox games at Fenway Park.

Swimming with them.

Answering their questions about God.

Taking my daughters to the ballet.

Watching them build forts out of chairs, tables, and blankets in the living room.

Running 5Ks and 10Ks with them, and seeing them along the course when I run my marathons.

Going to parent-teacher conferences.

Watching Little League games.

Attending religious services with my children and seeing them pray.

Getting medallions from them in AA meetings on my sober birthdays.

Going to the movies.

Going to professional sports events—baseball, football, college basketball, college hockey.

Taking walks.

Playing *The Beatles: Rock Band* on Wii.

Watching *Phineas and Ferb* with them (if you haven't seen it, it's brilliant).

Watching my sons learn to ride a unicycle, juggle, perform magic, and do other things that I could never do.

Going shoe shopping and dress shopping with my daughters.

Celebrating work successes with them.

Attending their school assemblies when they're getting awards for student of the month or whatever.

Taking them on vacations.

Seeing them interact with my mom, who just turned eighty and lives nearby.

Watching my boys laugh uncontrollably when I tell them a good joke.

Seeing them get along.

I could go on and on, but I think you get the point. *The price of admission to all of this is the willingness to open yourself up to the kind of fear, frustration, pain, and ultimately growth that the transition to fatherhood requires.* But without a doubt, my friend, it's the best ride in the park.

As I mentioned, I have deep regrets about the moments when I lost my temper and yelled at them or at my wife. I'm hardly a perfect person, and don't let the fancy clothes fool you—I'm still an alcoholic. But if you were to ask my children how I feel about them, I'm certain that each of the four of them would tell you, unequivocally, that I love them beyond words. Or, as we used to say to each other when they were three and four years old, that I love them more than space.

The world seems worse today than when I was growing up. Certainly, we had the fear of the Soviets and the atom bomb, and I do remember the duck and cover drills, when we grade-school children would practice hiding under our desks to protect ourselves from nuclear attack. (A lot of good that would have done.)

Today, though, the world seems colder, more threatening, more divisive, less nurturing, more economically divided.

That's why it's more essential than ever to make the home an oasis of safety, good feeling, and love. That's what I get to do every day, and that's what I know you will do as well.

There are subjects I haven't touched on in this book because I simply have no experience with them. I haven't said anything about blended families, for example, because my experience is limited. I just don't know anything about them from the inside.

I haven't touched on issues like sexual abuse, because I'm not a professional, and it's not something I know very much about. I also haven't talked much about becoming an empty nester, or dealing with the sorts of problems that older children can get into. I have to plead ignorance. I'm not there yet, and I'm hoping that my kids somehow skate past the really big problems that young people, myself included back in the day, can find. And as the Al-Anon book *One Day at a Time* says, "Never trouble till trouble troubles you."[19]

So in that sense, this book has its limitations, because I cannot speak with the weight of training and experience that you might find in other books.

To compensate, I've tried to be as relentlessly honest as I can about my own experiences, my own shortcomings, and my own growth as I have sought to usher the four young people God entrusted to my wife's and my care into our world. My hope for my children is that they will help counter the gloom and darkness that seems to be with us in these complicated times, and that is my wish for you and your family as well.

I now see fatherhood as the greatest challenge in my life, the Everest to climb, a day at a time—once I was able to summit my own issues of addiction, pain, and loss. I hope it will be that way for you. Children are fabulous. I found that after we had ours, I fell in love with all of them. I fell in love with being a parent, and all it means. All children want is love, attention, and a chance. You have been placed in a position to influence one or more small human beings and guide them, by word and deed, through the phases of childhood and into their own adult lives. As the Big Book says in a slightly different context, it is an experience you will not want to miss.

Keep your eyes open, be loving, get good help, and have fun. You are in for the ride of your life.

Some Notes
from What You Just Read

1. Terry Gorski, audio recordings from talks, circulated in the 1990s.

2. Warren Farrell, *Why Men Are the Way They Are* (New York: Berkley, 1988).

3. John Gray, *Men Are from Mars, Women Are from Venus: The Classic Guide to Understanding the Opposite Sex* (New York: Harper, 2012).

4. Chuck C., *A New Pair of Glasses,* 3rd ed. (Irvine, CA: New-Look, 2003).

5. John Grey, *Relationship Tools for Positive Change: How to Transform Issues or Upsets into Opportunities to Strengthen Love* (Sebastopol, CA: Leap Frog Press, 2005).

6. Harville Hendrix, *Getting the Love You Want: A Guide for Couples, 20th Anniversary Edition* (New York: Henry Holt & Co., 2007).

7. Meyer Friedman and Ray Rosenman, *Type A Behavior and Your Heart* (New York: Knopf, 1974).

8. As told to author.

9. The Earl Nightingale audio collection is very vast. And I encourage you to listen to all of it. This quote is in there, somewhere. After all, Earl's main message was "We become what we think about."

10. I've had the pleasure of hearing the Rabbi speak many times. This is something he's shared in a speech.

11. Richard Kirshenbaum, *Isn't That Rich? Life Among the 1%* (New York: Open Road Media, 2015).

12. Michael Medved, *Hollywood vs. America: Popular Culture and the War on Traditional Values* (New York: Harper Collins, 1992).

13. Paul Reiser, *Babyhood* (New York: William Morrow, 1997). I know what you're thinking—when does this guy have all this time to read all these books? The short answer is I haven't slept since 1996.

14. Wendy Mogel, *The Blessing of a Skinned Knee: Using Jewish Teachings to Raise Self-Reliant Children* (New York: Scribner, 2001).

15. Tim Donaghy, *Personal Foul: A First-Person Account of the Scandal that Rocked the NBA* (Four Daughters LLC: 2010).

16. Erma Bombeck, *The Erma Bombeck Collection: If Life Is a Bowl of Cherries, What Am I Doing in the Pits?, Motherhood, and The Grass Is Always Greener Over the Septic Tank* (New York: Open Road Media, 2013).

17. *Alcoholics Anonymous,* 4th ed. (New York: Alcoholics Anonymous World Services, 2001).

18. Adele Faber and Elaine Mazlish, *How to Talk So Kids Will Listen & Listen So Kids Will Talk* (New York: Scribner, 2012).

19. *One Day at a Time in Al-Anon* (New York: Al-Anon Family Group Headquarters, 1987).

Some Acknowledgments

First, my wife and kids, for their patience and tolerance.

Next, Vanessa Torrado—the dream editor. She saw one of my manuscripts and decided, "I found my guy." Well, this guy found his perfect publishing partner and I could not be more grateful.

And then, to the rest of the Hazelden team, because thanks to them, I'm a better writer than I really am: The very excellent production manager Heather Silsbee; copyeditor extraordinaire Betty Christiansen; Susan Whitten and Emily Reller, marketing geniuses; Wendy Videen, who ensures these books don't just get made, but get made fabulously; and finally the exceptionally talented design director Terri Kinne.

And also, my sponsors, friends, and sponsees in my various Twelve Step programs. I'd name you all, but I don't want to blow your anonymity.

Finally, Bill W. and Dr. Bob, who had the gift of desperation and gave us all the gift of a second (or third or fourth or fifth) chance at life.

About Sober Dad

"Michael Graubart" is a longtime sober member of Alcoholics Anonymous, has been a member of Al-Anon for decades, and attends Overeaters Anonymous meetings as well. As he says, "If it moves, I'm obsessed with it, and if it stands still, I'm addicted to it." A *New York Times* best-selling author, Michael is married and the father of four children. He writes under a pseudonym to maintain his anonymity and speak frankly about his experiences in Twelve Step recovery.

Keep up with Sober Dad online.
He has a blog and is all over the social-sphere.
#SoberDad

About Hazelden Publishing

As part of the Hazelden Betty Ford Foundation, Hazelden Publishing offers both cutting-edge educational resources and inspirational books. Our print and digital works help guide individuals in treatment and recovery, and their loved ones. Professionals who work to prevent and treat addiction also turn to Hazelden Publishing for evidence-based curricula, digital content solutions, and videos for use in schools, treatment programs, correctional programs, and electronic health records systems. We also offer training for implementation of our curricula.

Through published and digital works, Hazelden Publishing extends the reach of healing and hope to individuals, families, and communities affected by addiction and related issues.

For more information about Hazelden publications,
please call **800-328-9000**
or visit us online at **hazelden.org/bookstore**.

Other titles that may interest you:

A Sober Mom's Guide to Recovery
Taking Care of Yourself to Take Care of Your Kids
ROSEMARY O'CONNOR
Rosemary O'Connor brings her many years of experience working with women in recovery to addressing the key life issues mothers face at all stages of their recovery path.
Order No. 7938, also available as an e-book

Touchstones
A Book of Daily Meditations for Men
Speaking straight to men who are striving for serenity or trying to maintain emotionally and spiritually balanced lives, these daily touchstones underscore the lessons of intimacy, integrity, and spirituality.
Order No. 5029, also available as an e-book

Recovering My Kid
Parenting Young Adults in Treatment and Beyond
JOSEPH LEE, MD
National expert Dr. Joseph Lee explains the nature of youth addiction and treatment and how families can create a safe and supportive environment for their loved ones during treatment and throughout their recovery.
Order No. 4693, also available as an e-book

• • •

Hazelden Publishing books are available at fine bookstores everywhere. To order from Hazelden Publishing, call **800-328-9000** or visit **hazelden.org/bookstore**.